Performers

by Marie Prince

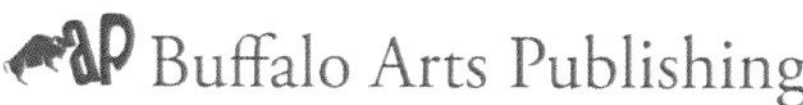 Buffalo Arts Publishing

For information, address Buffalo Arts Publishing, 179 Greenfield Drive, Tonawanda, NY 14150

Email: info@buffaloartspublishing.com

ISBN 978-1-950006-11-3

About the Artist

Marie Prince resides in Williamsville and works primarily in acrylic, collage, and watercolor. She received her Bachelors and Masters Degrees from Buffalo State College. She concluded a career in the public sector and is presently pursing her artistic passions full time. Her work has won wide acclaim in juried competition and is included in many private collections.

To inquire about any of the works contained in this book, please email Marie Prince at:

email: artmprince@yahoo.com
or
telephone: (716) 634-7015

Contents

My series is a tribute to performers of all types that make us happy, sad, aware, and/or just thoughtful. They entertain us and offer an escape to magic places that at times makes life worth living.

—Marie Prince
May, 2020

All in the Family

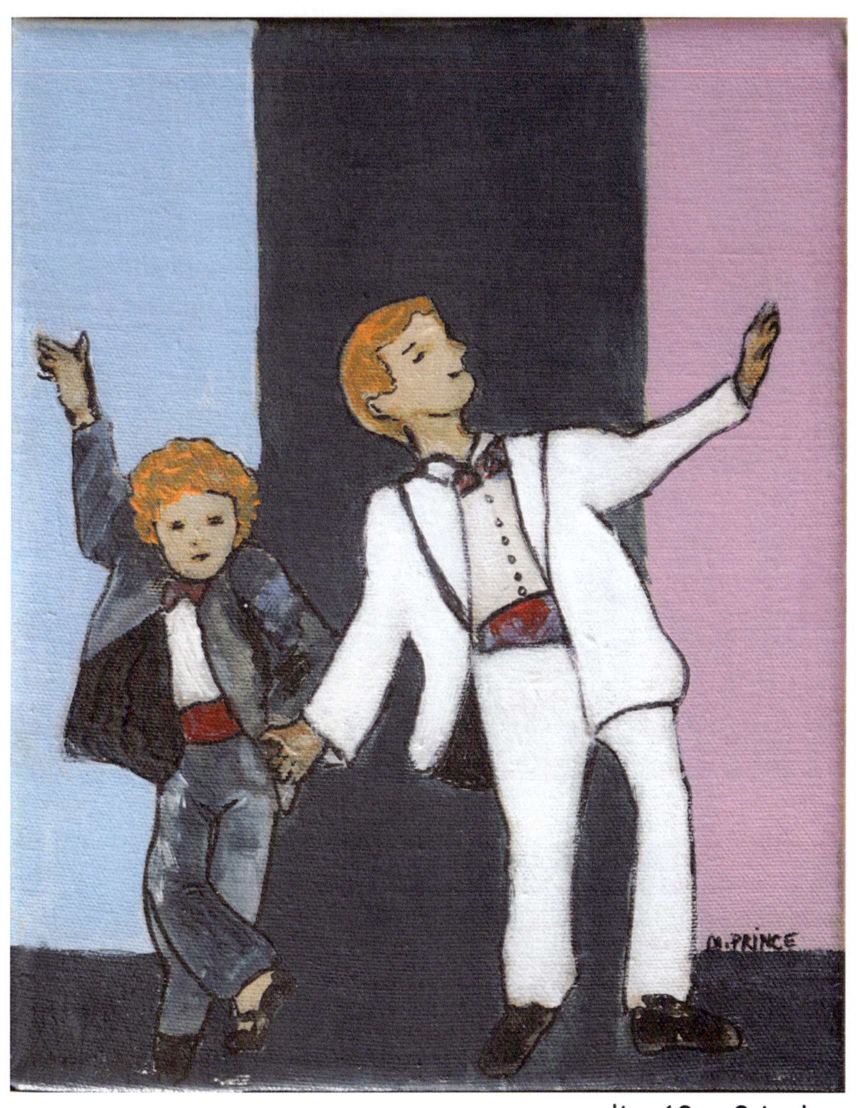

acrylic, 10 x 8 inches

Guitar

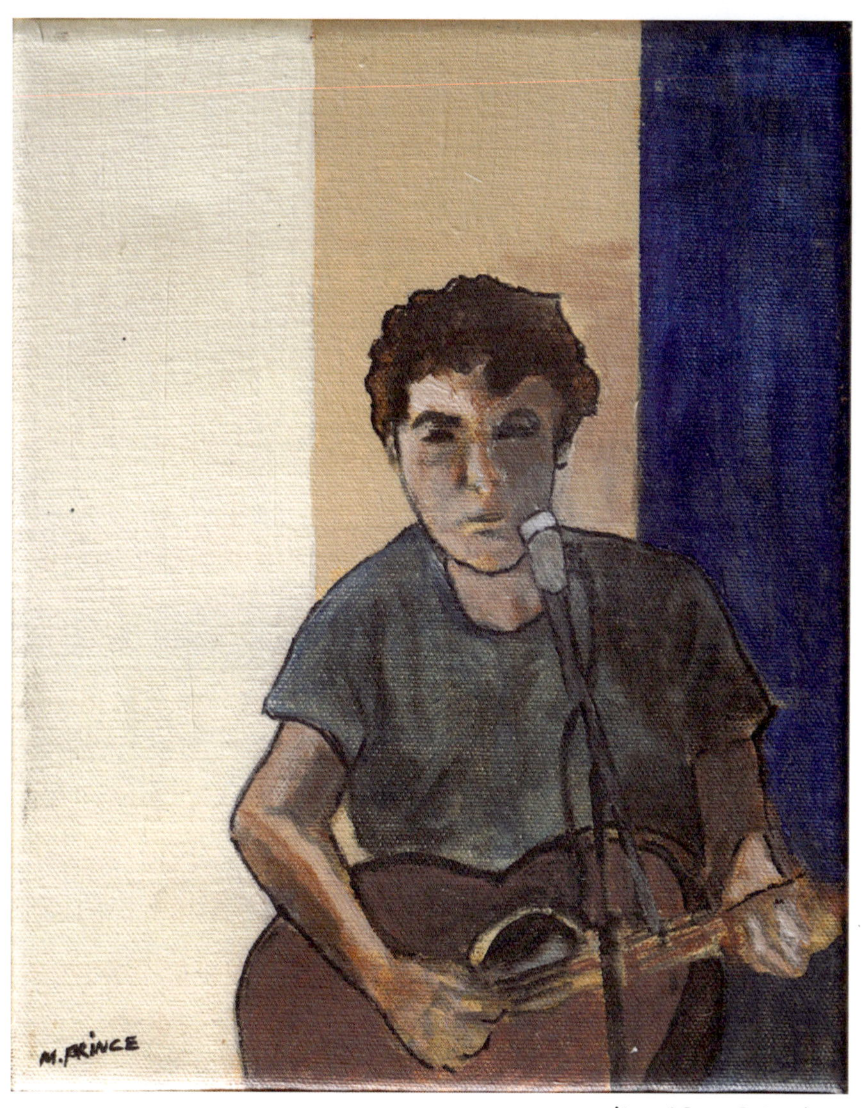

acrylic, 10 x 8 inches

Jump

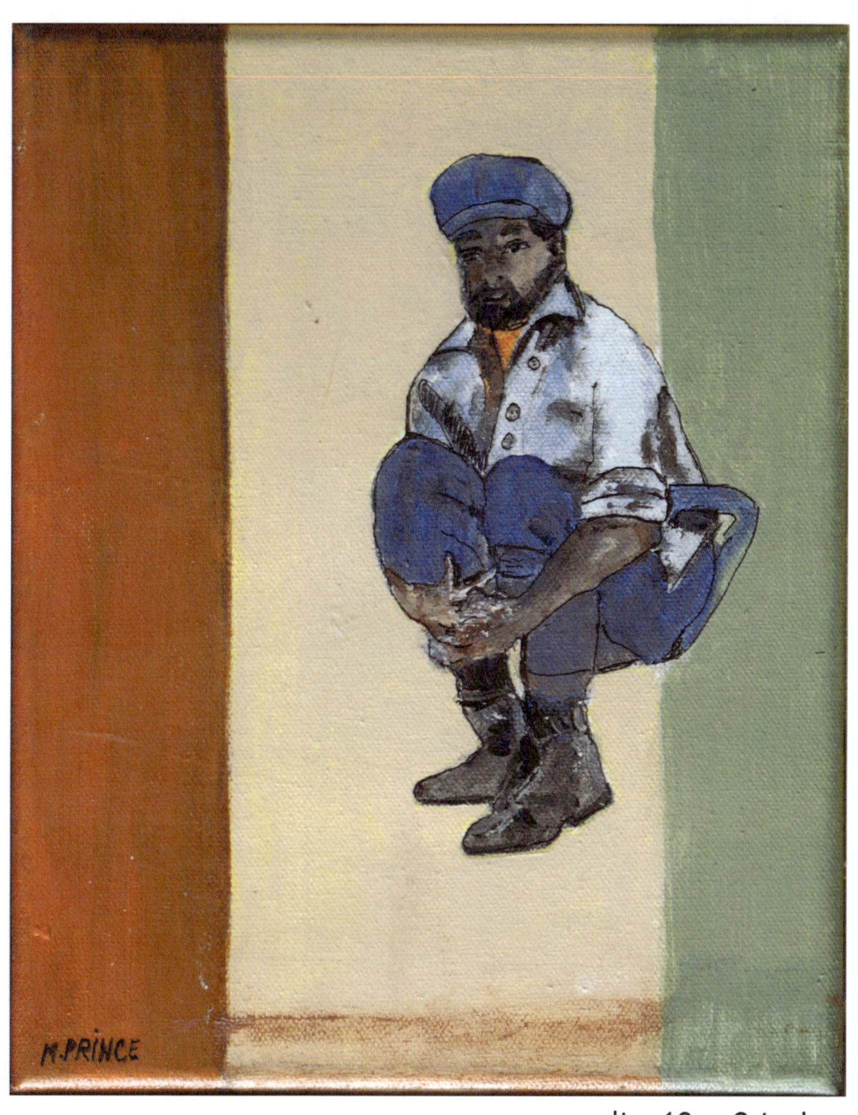

acrylic, 10 x 8 inches

On Her Toes

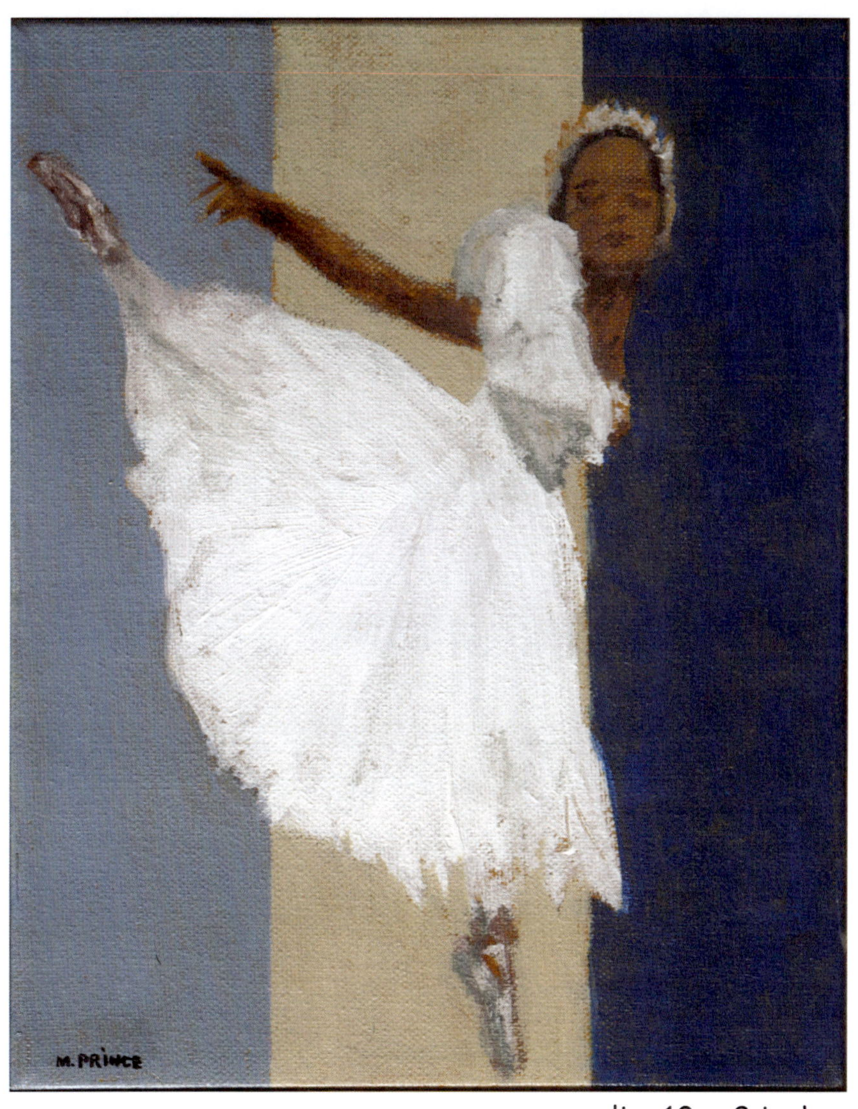

acrylic, 10 x 8 inches

Supporting Players

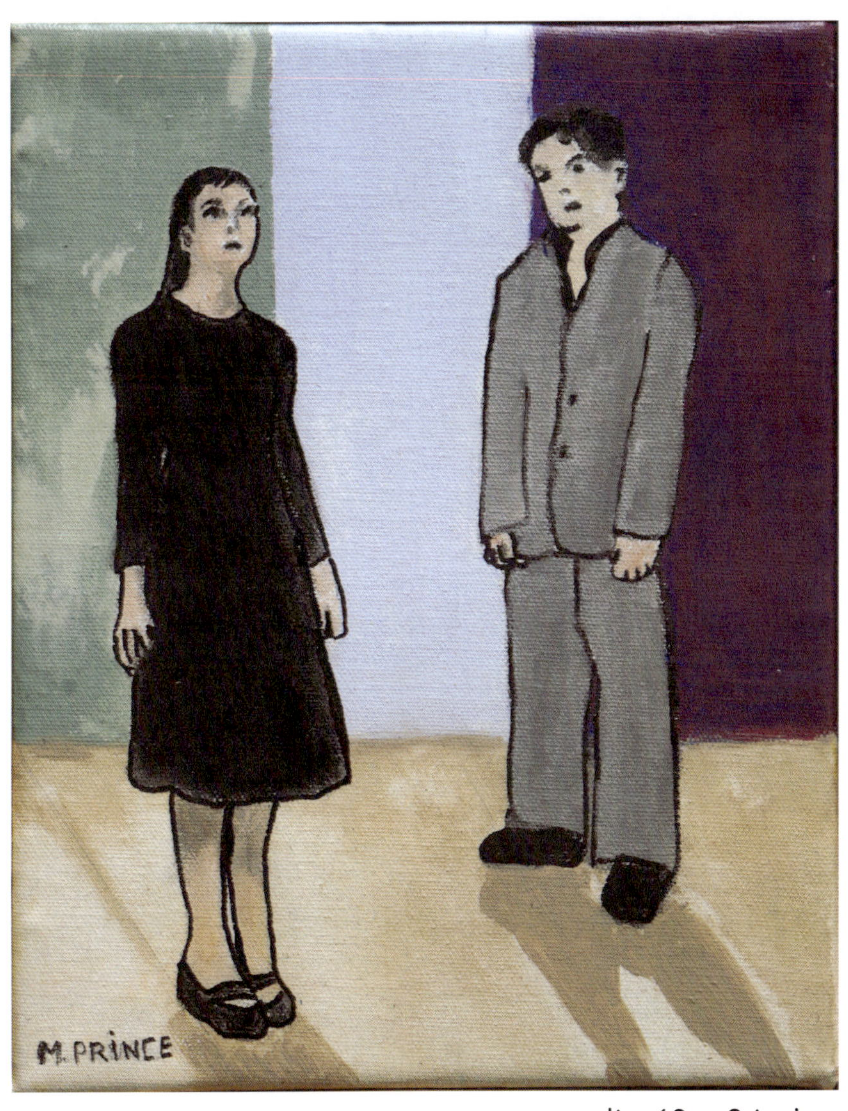

acrylic, 10 x 8 inches

Actors

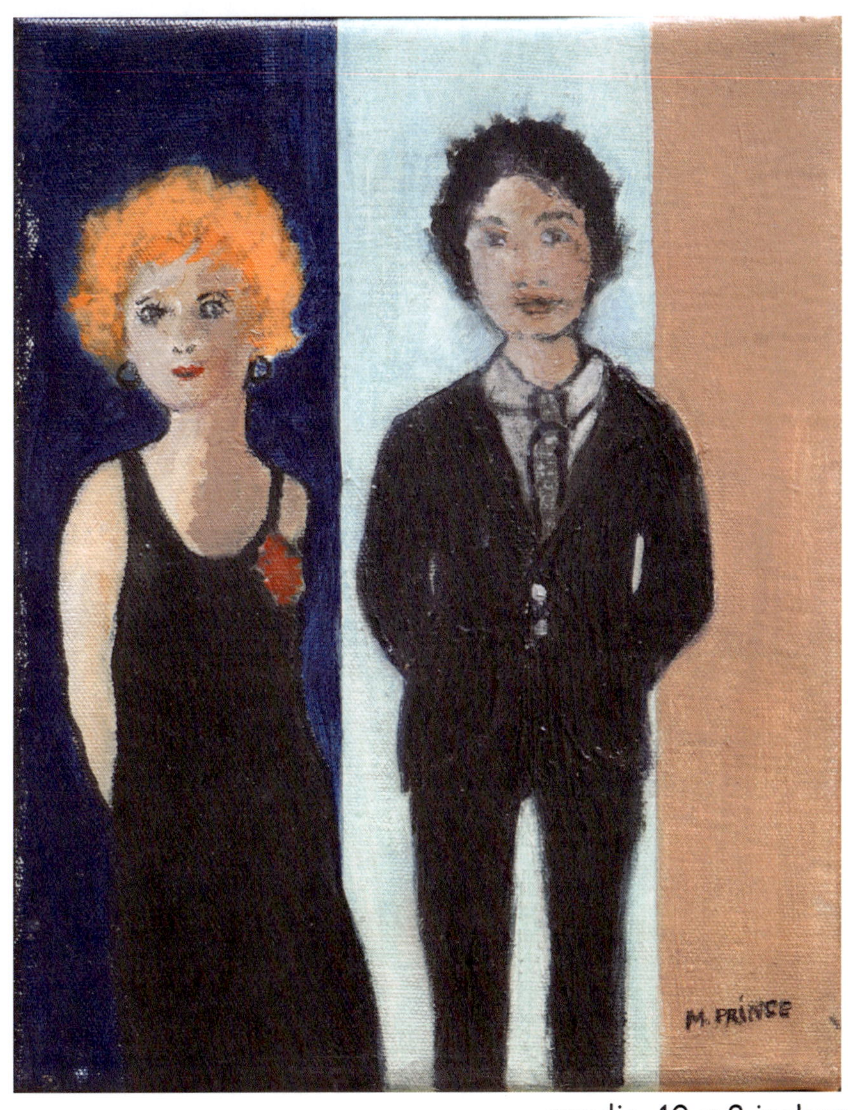

acrylic, 10 x 8 inches

On Her Toes II

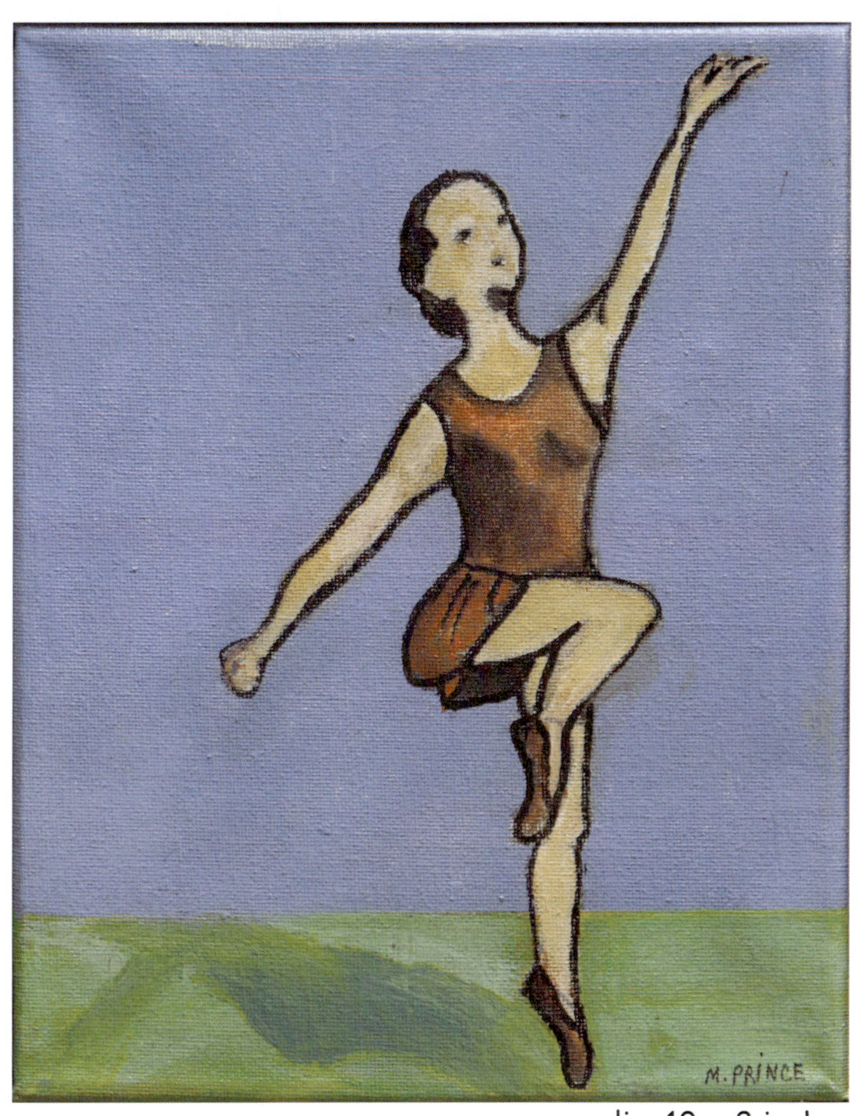

acrylic, 10 x 8 inches

The Hoofers

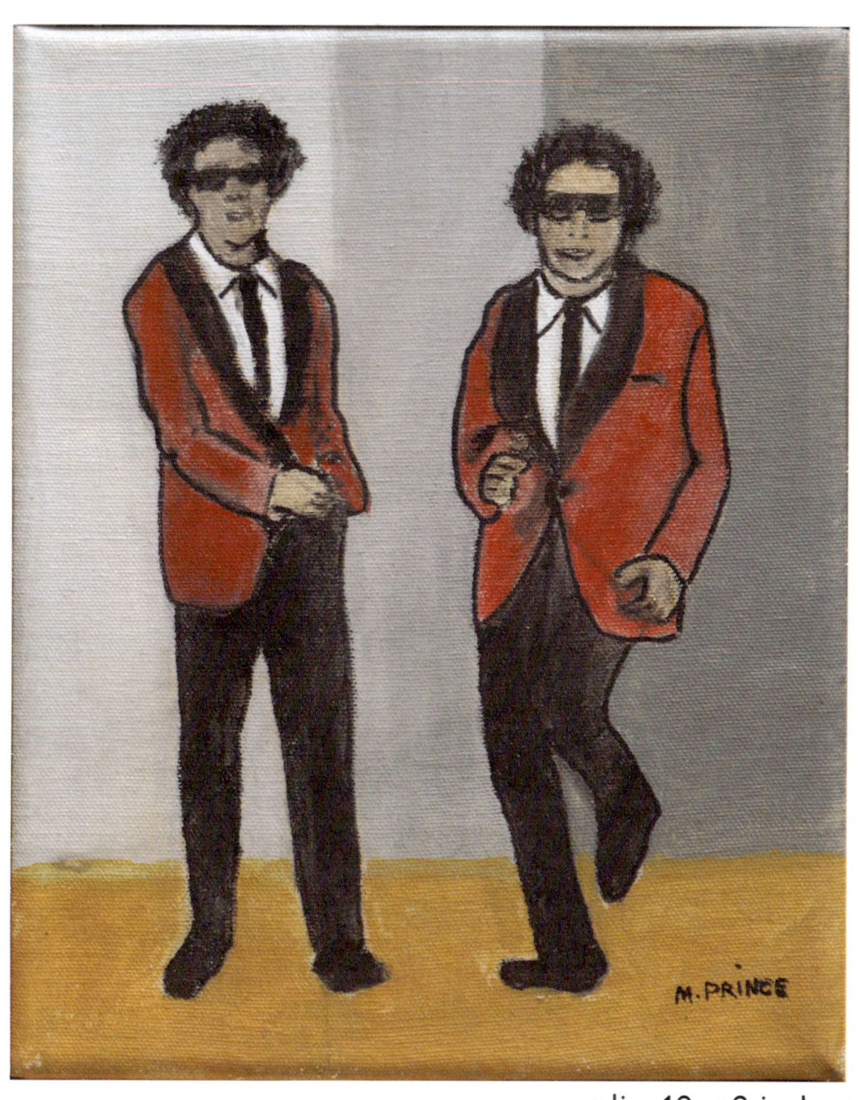

acrylic, 10 x 8 inches

Perfect Timing

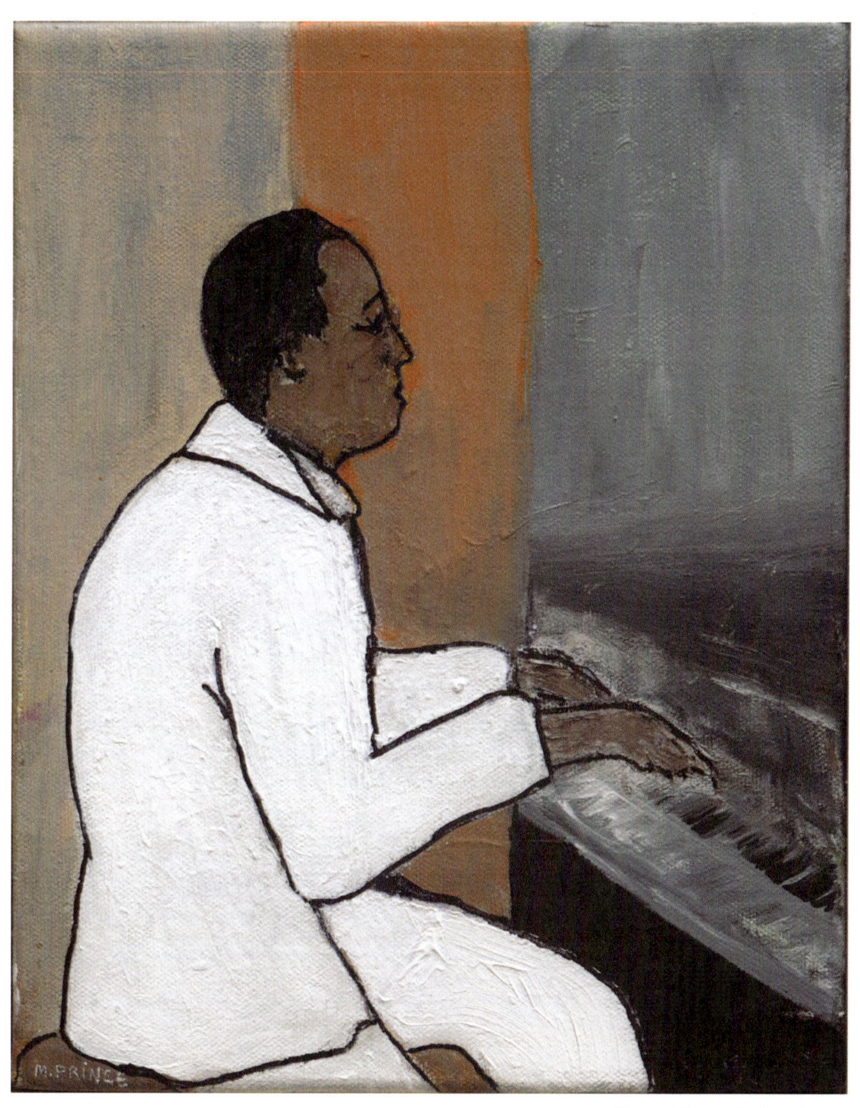

acrylic, 10 x 8 inches

First Act

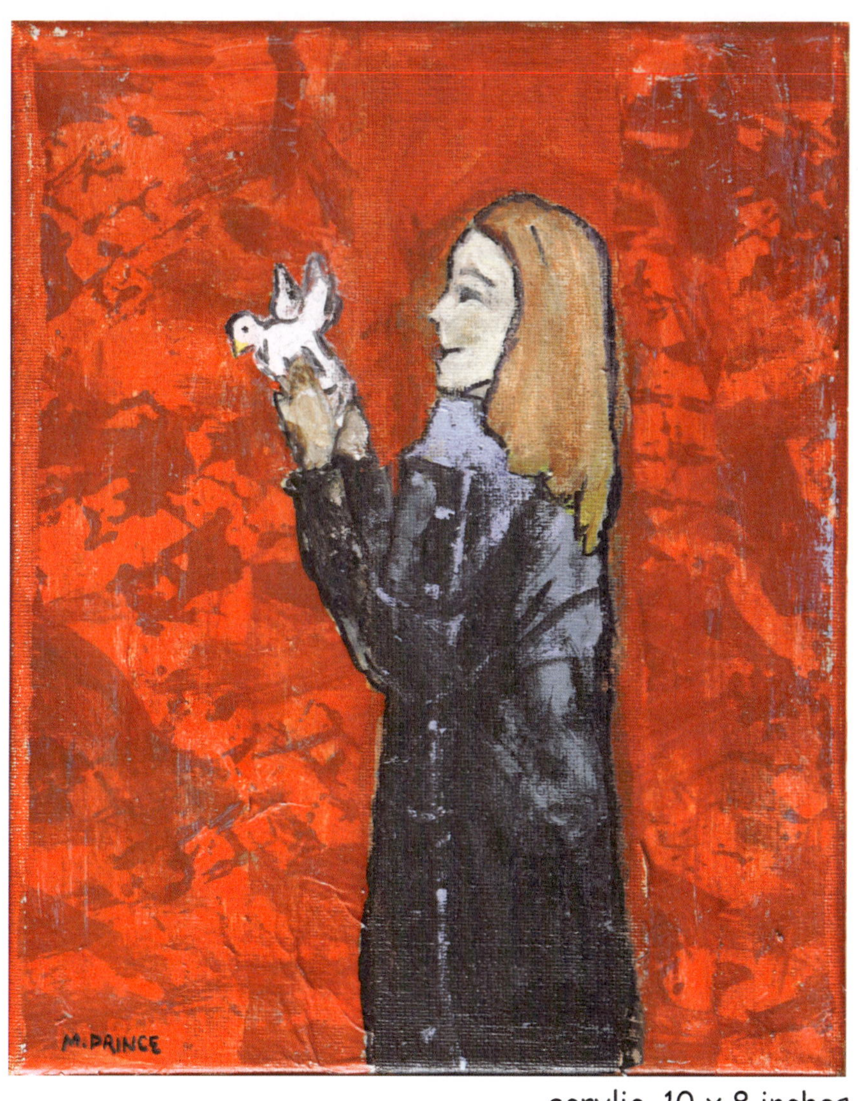

acrylic, 10 x 8 inches

Gospel Sounds

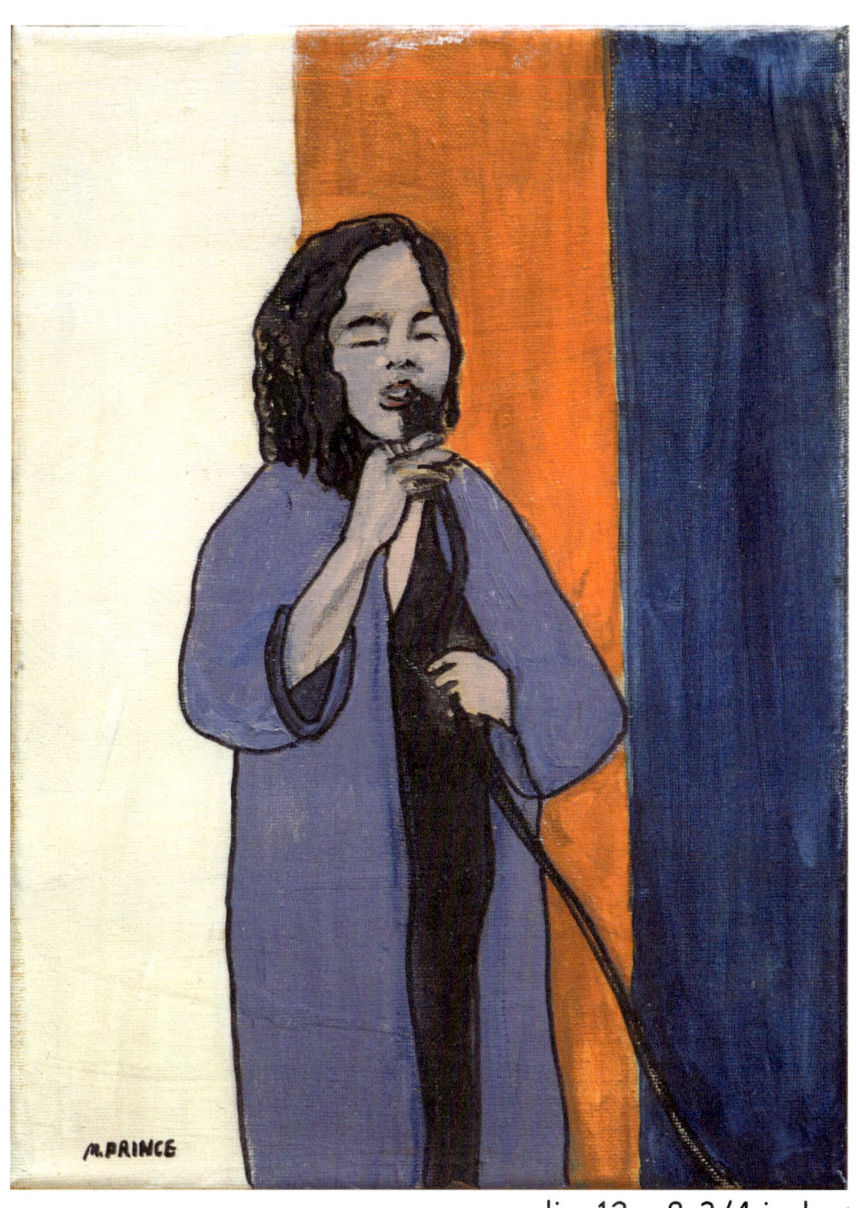

acrylic, 12 x 8-3/4 inches

Debut

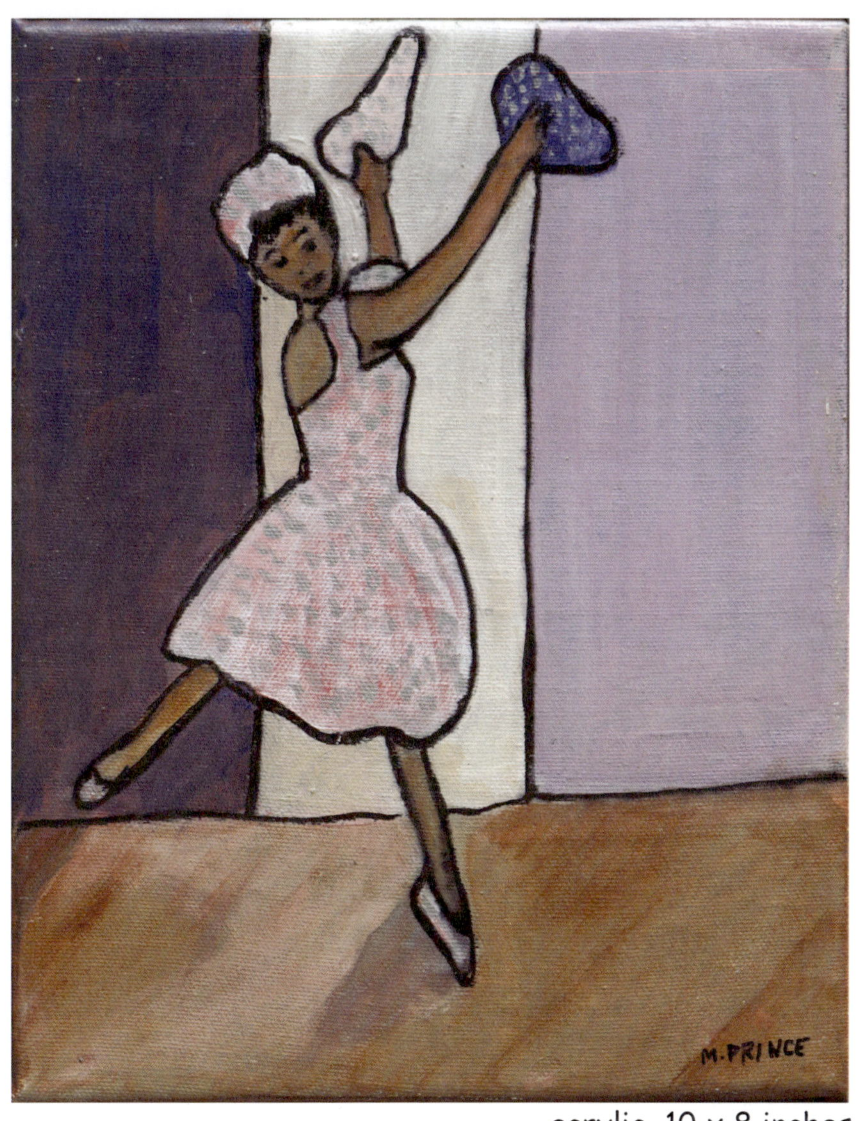

acrylic, 10 x 8 inches

Fast Stomping

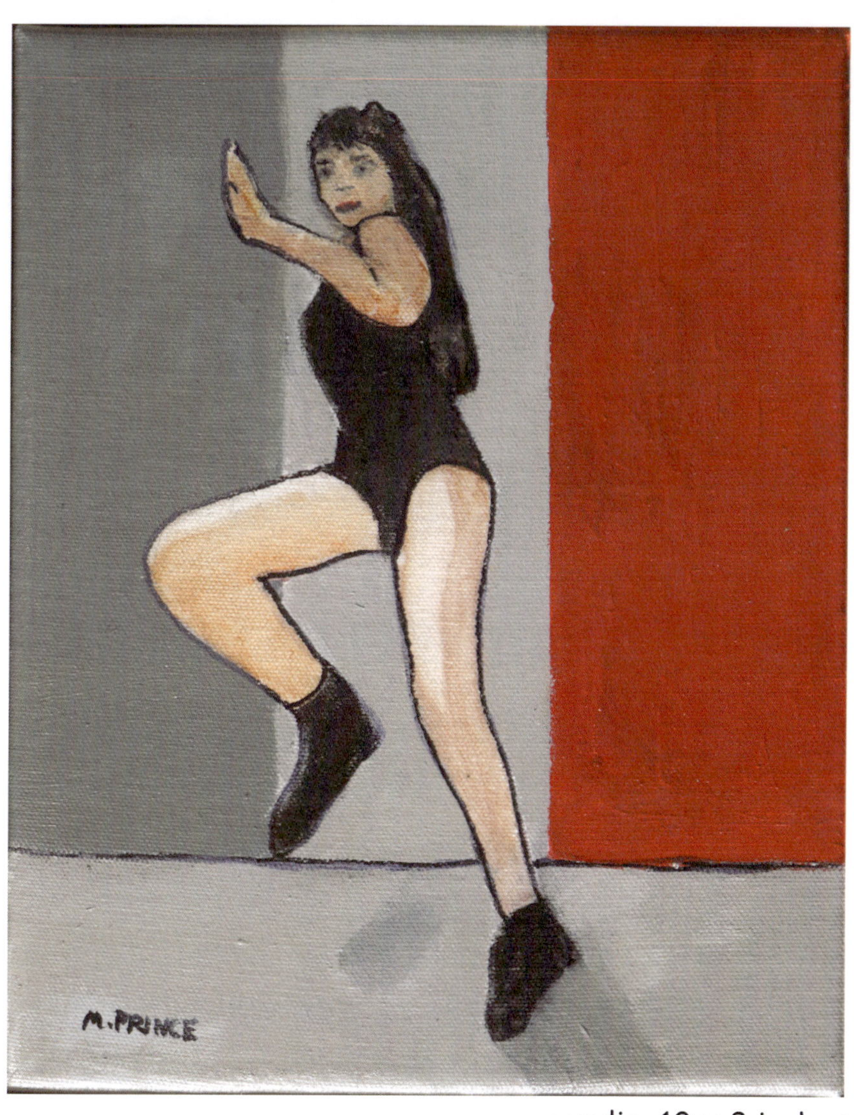

acrylic, 10 x 8 inches

Leading Lady

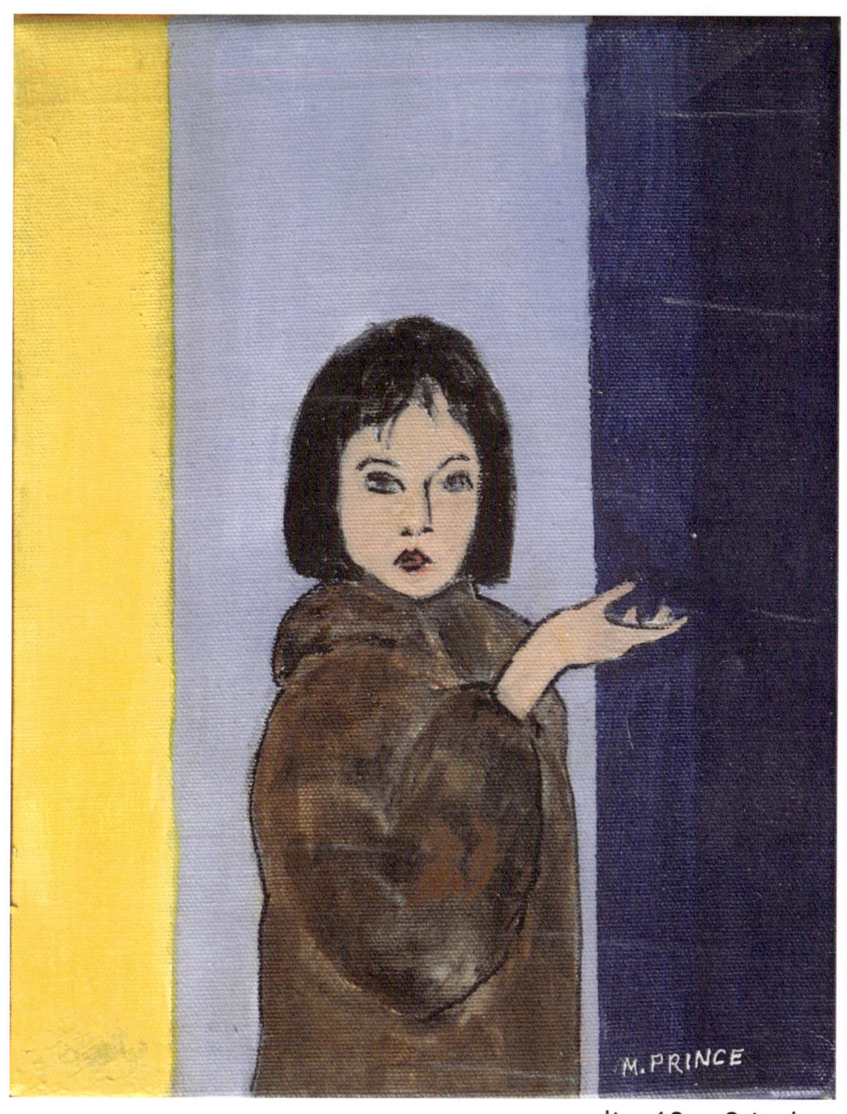

acrylic, 10 x 8 inches

Song

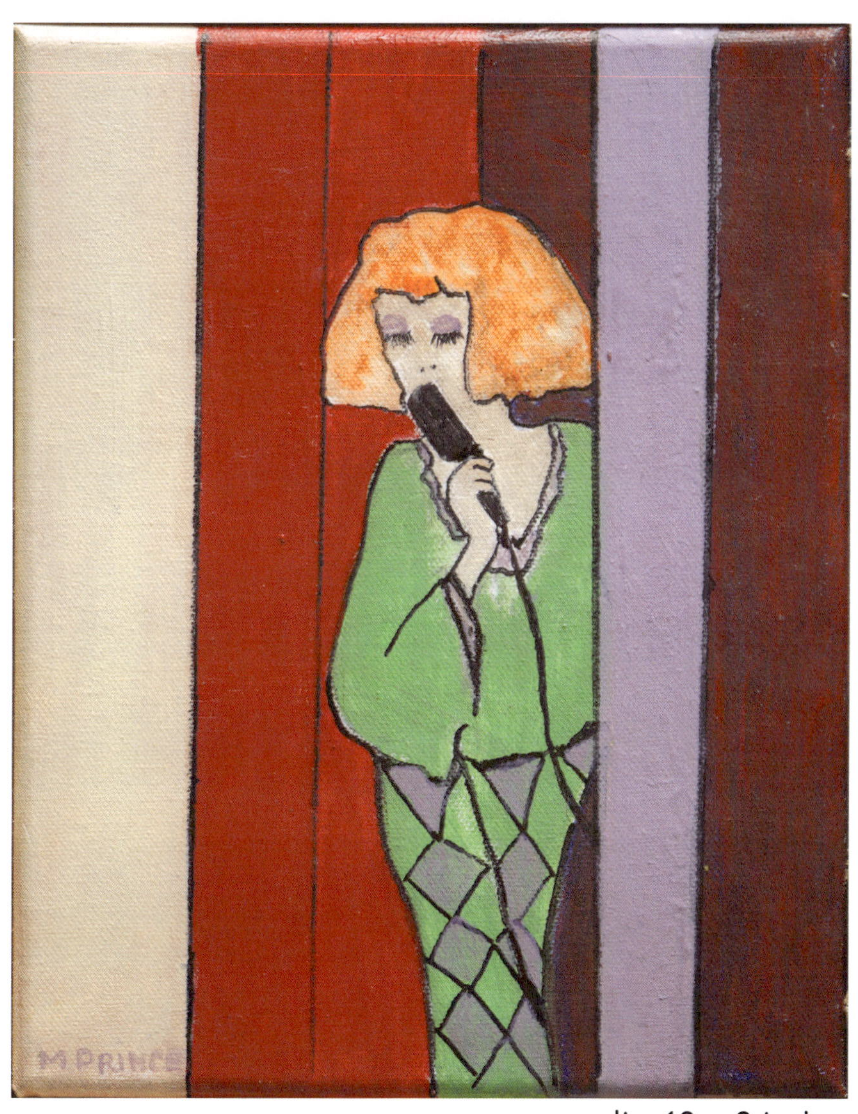

acrylic, 10 x 8 inches

Tryout

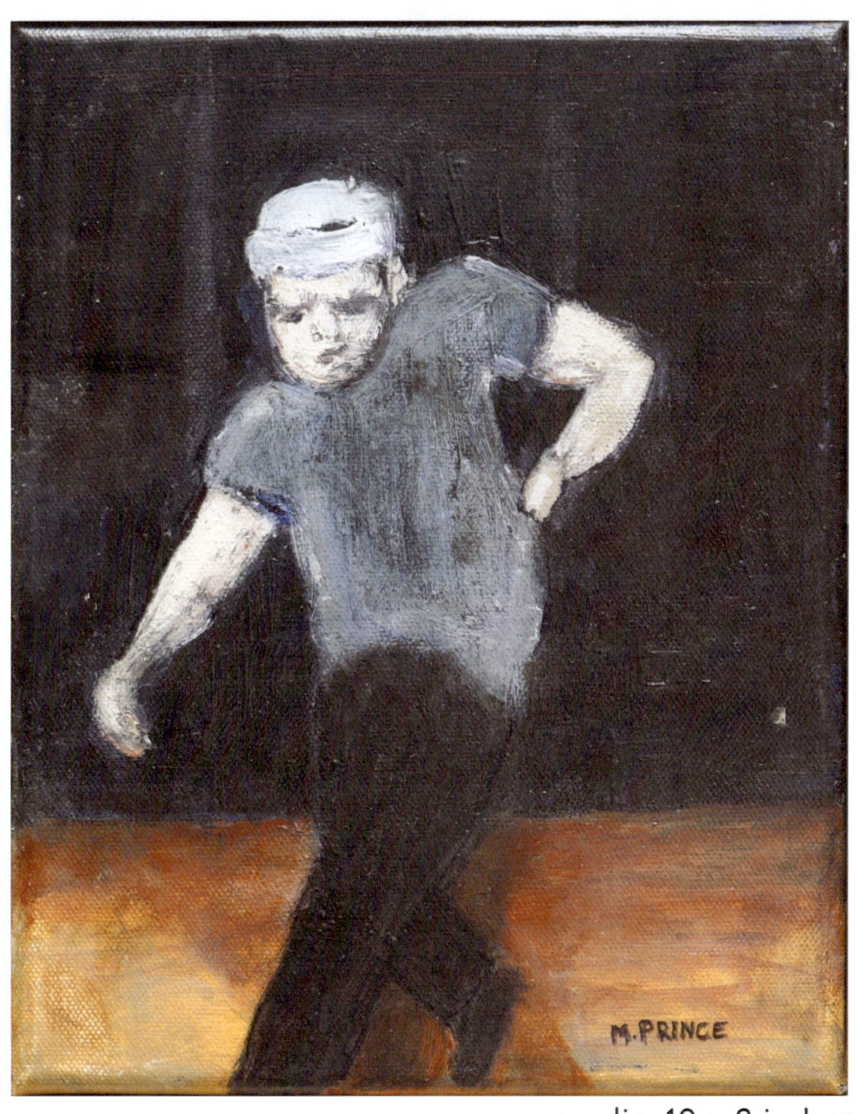

acrylic, 10 x 8 inches

Auditions
at
Noon

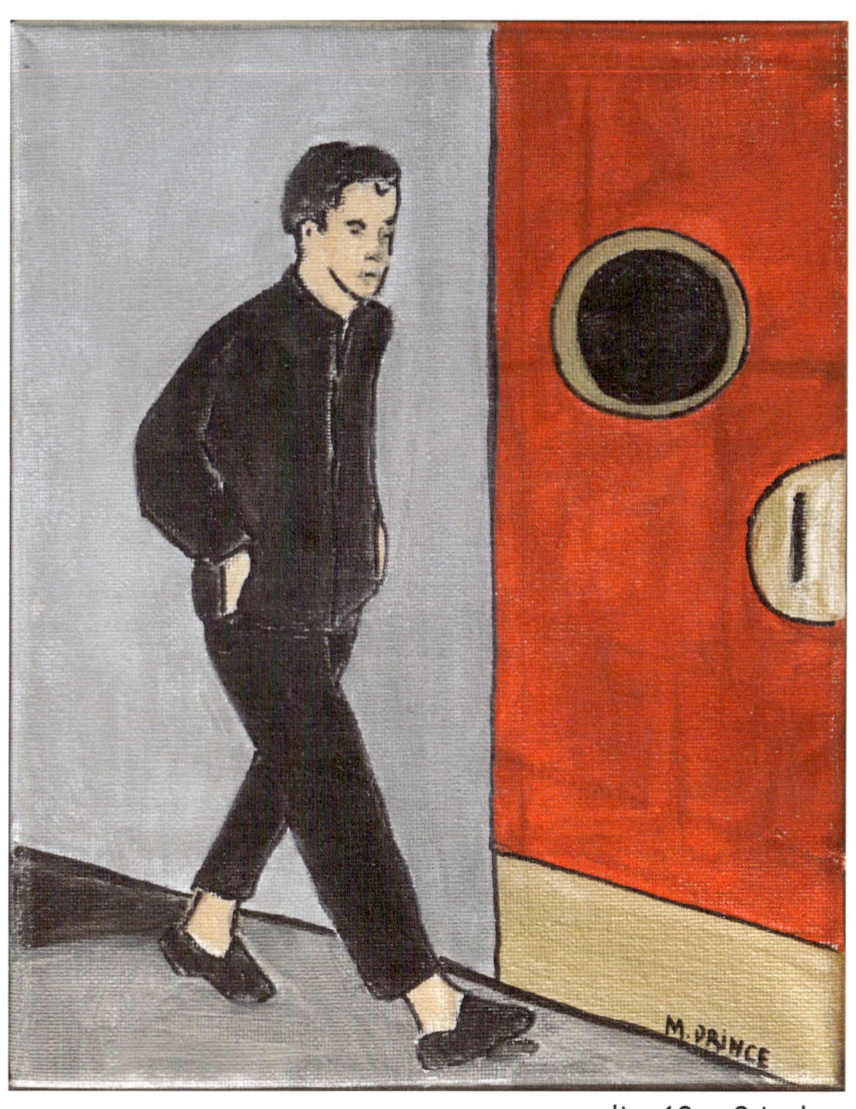

acrylic, 10 x 8 inches

Rehearsing Steps

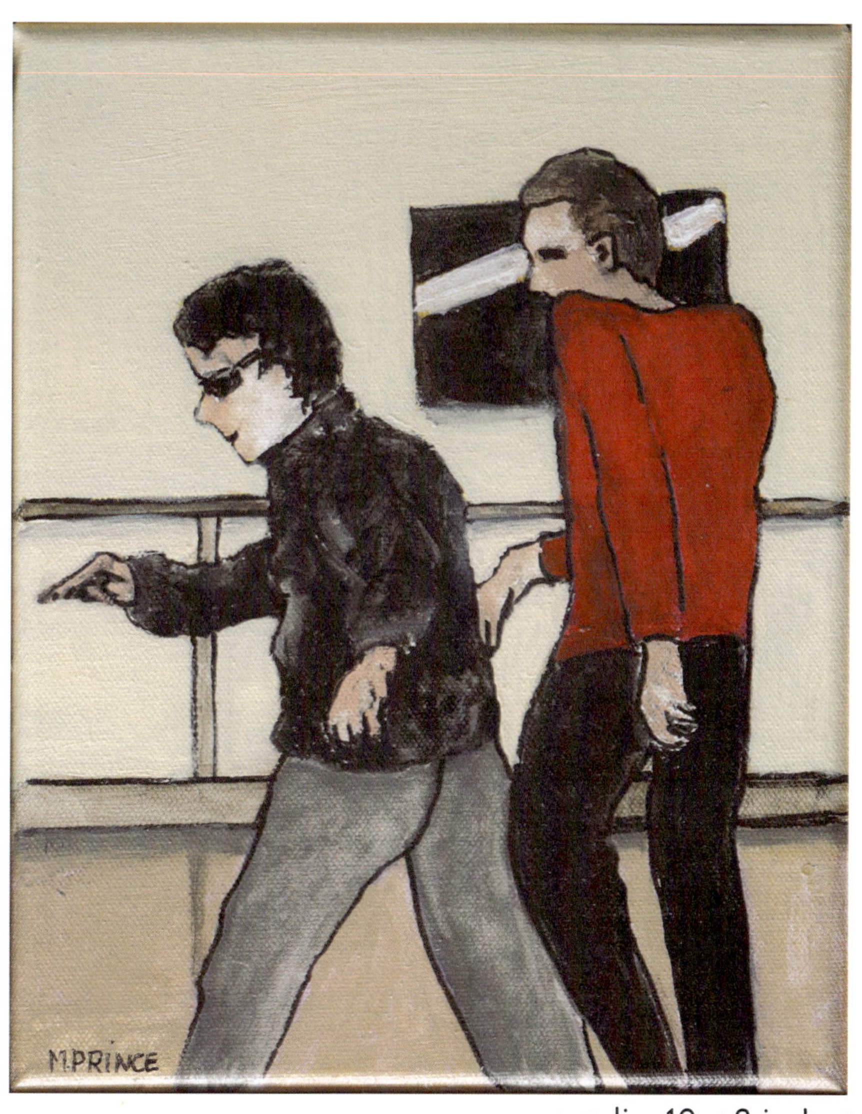

acrylic, 10 x 8 inches

Red DancingShoes

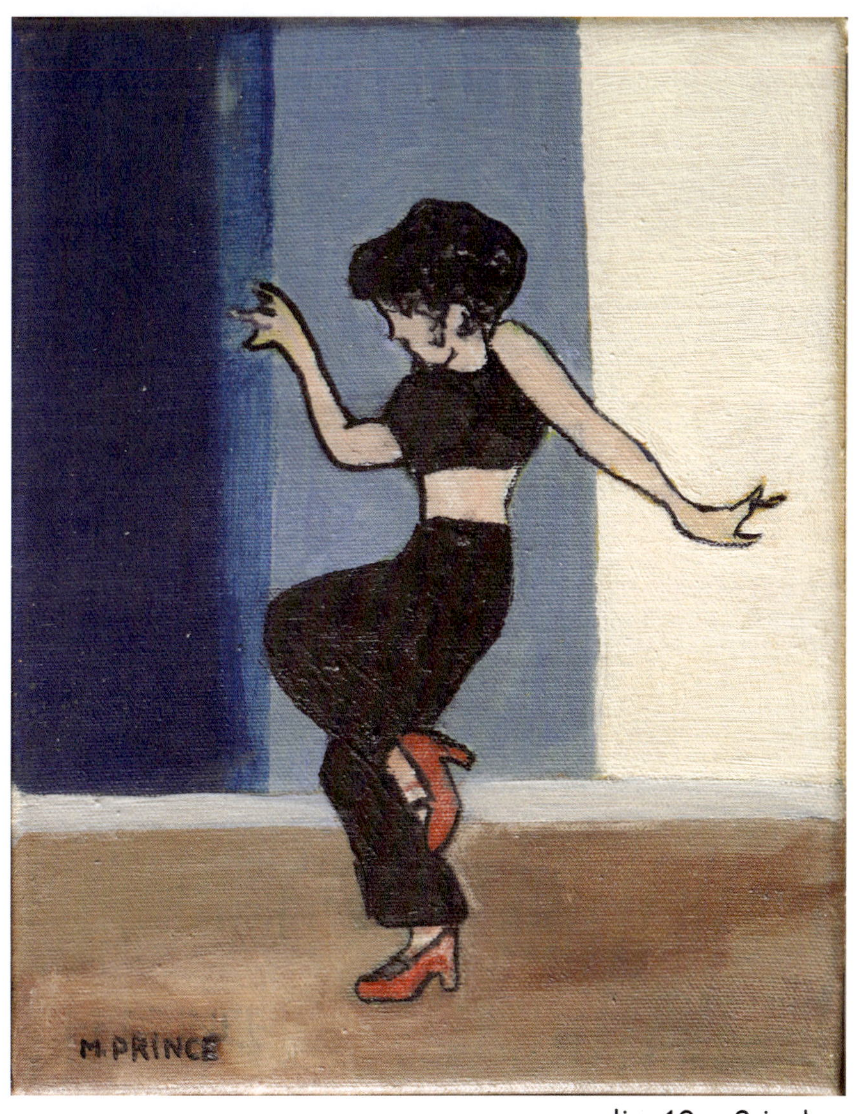

acrylic, 10 x 8 inches

Actors' Guild

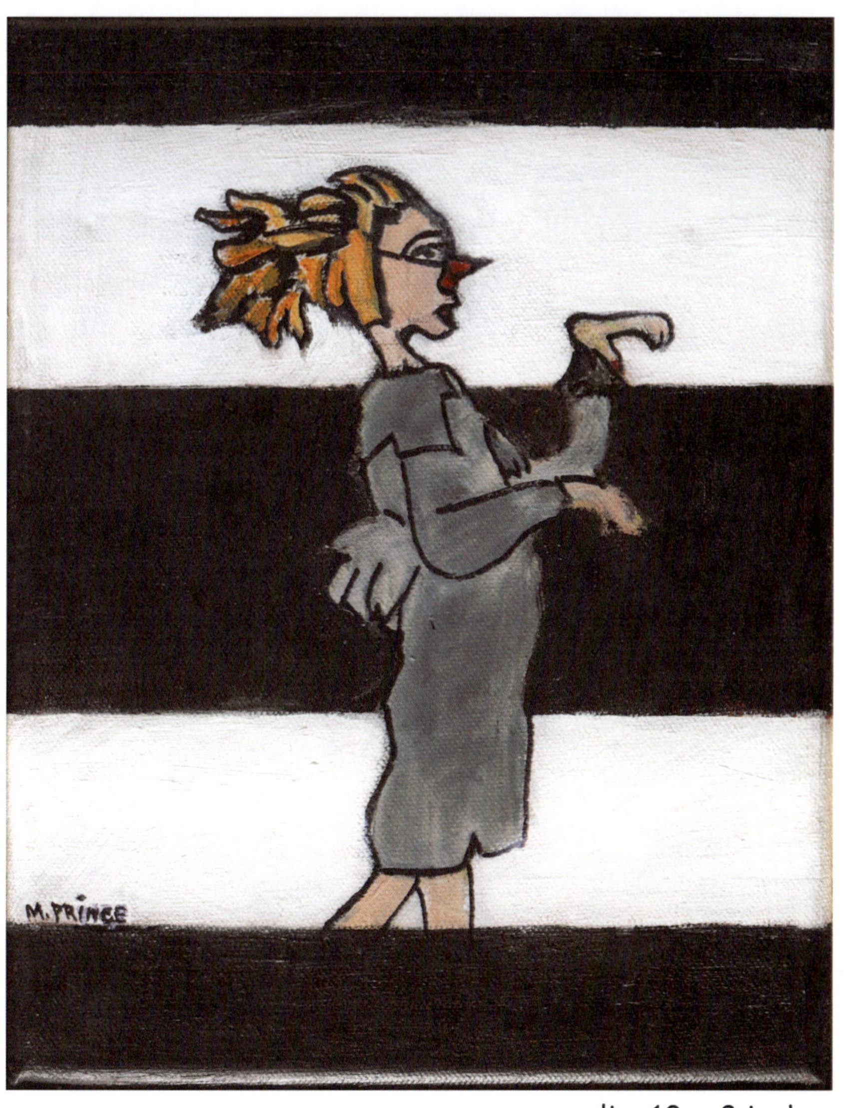

acrylic, 10 x 8 inches

Brass Trio

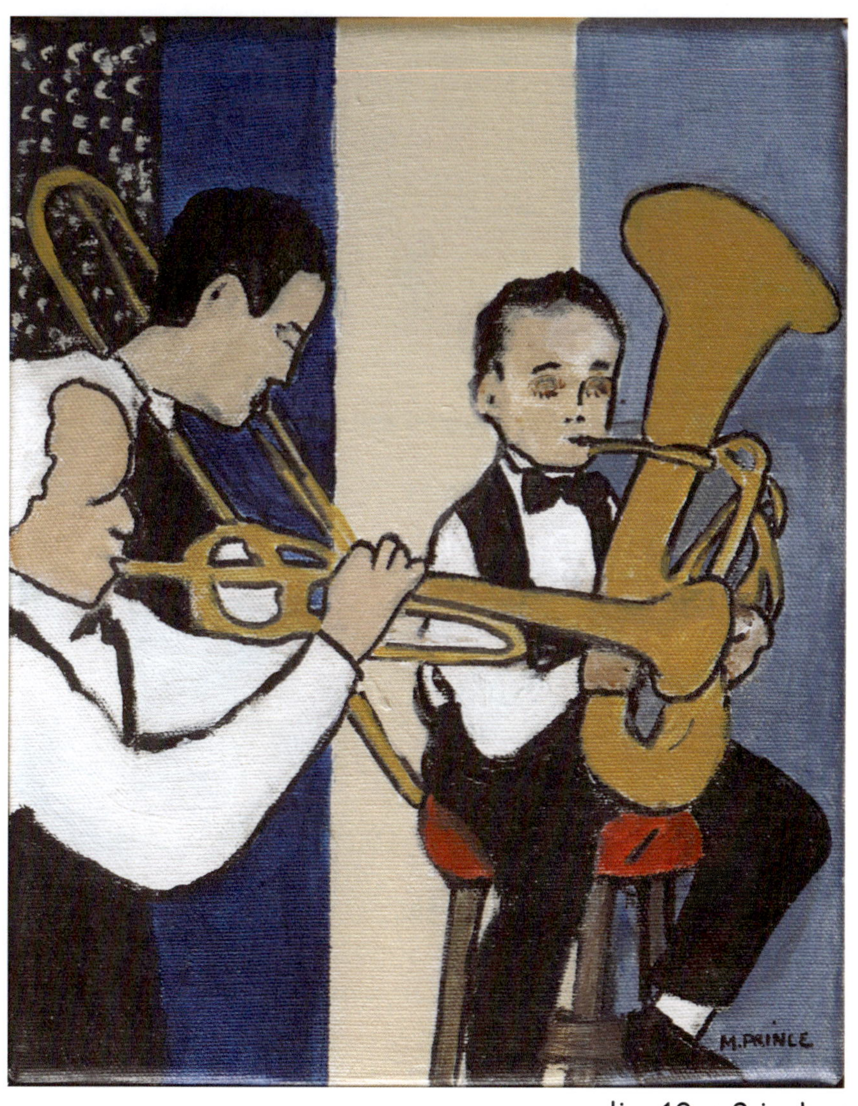

acrylic, 10 x 8 inches

Emergence

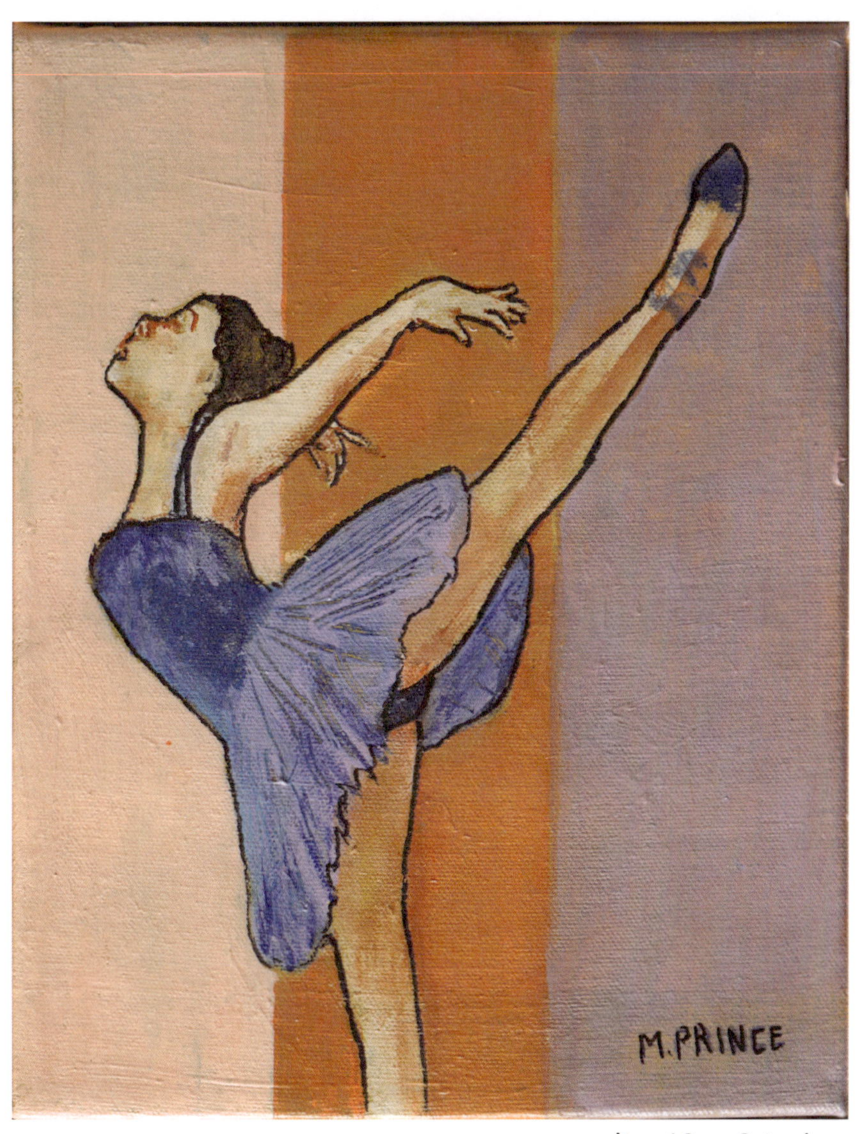

acrylic, 10 x 8 inches

Playing the Blues

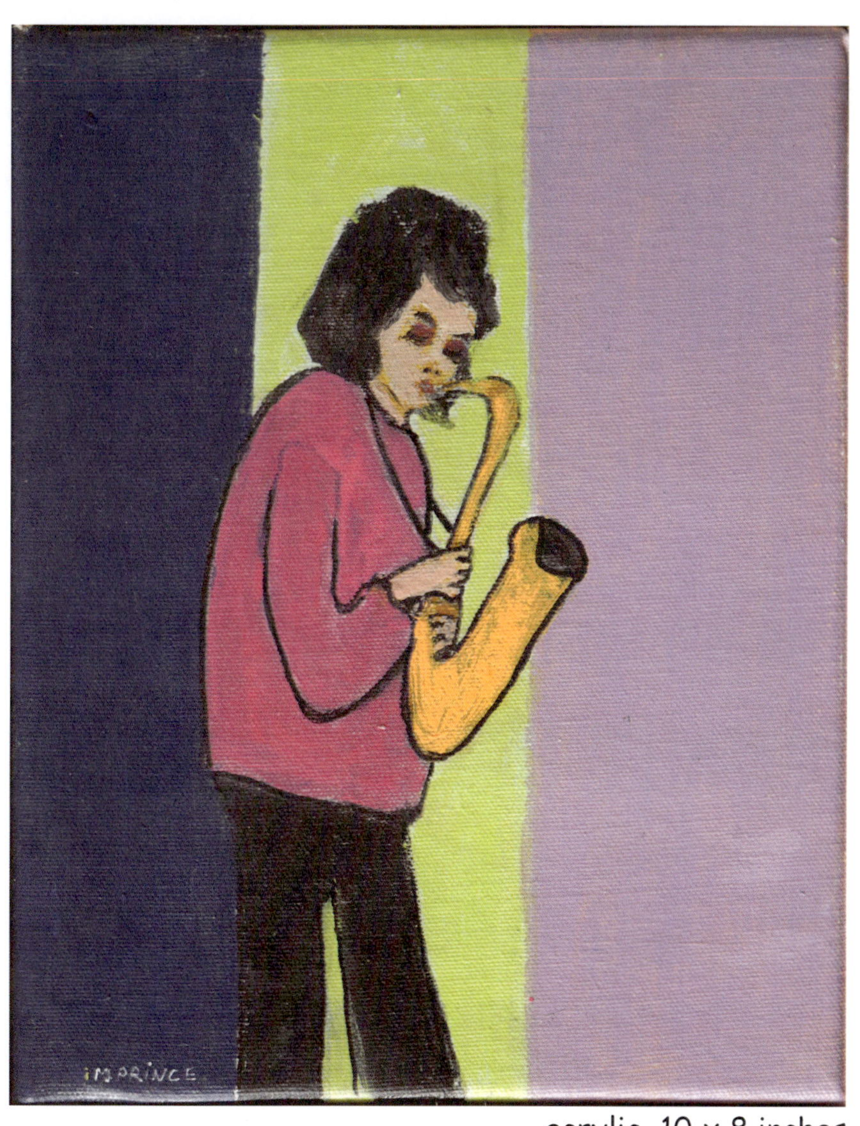

acrylic, 10 x 8 inches

Viola

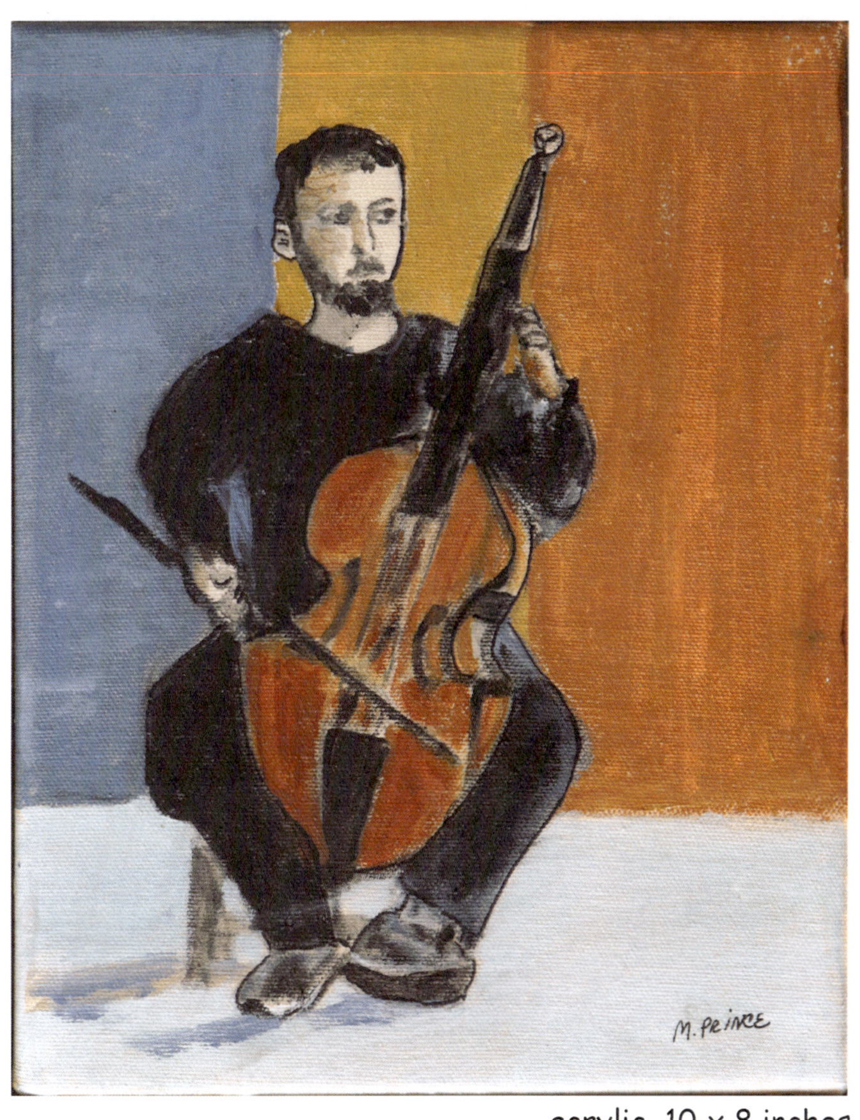

acrylic, 10 x 8 inches

One Man Show

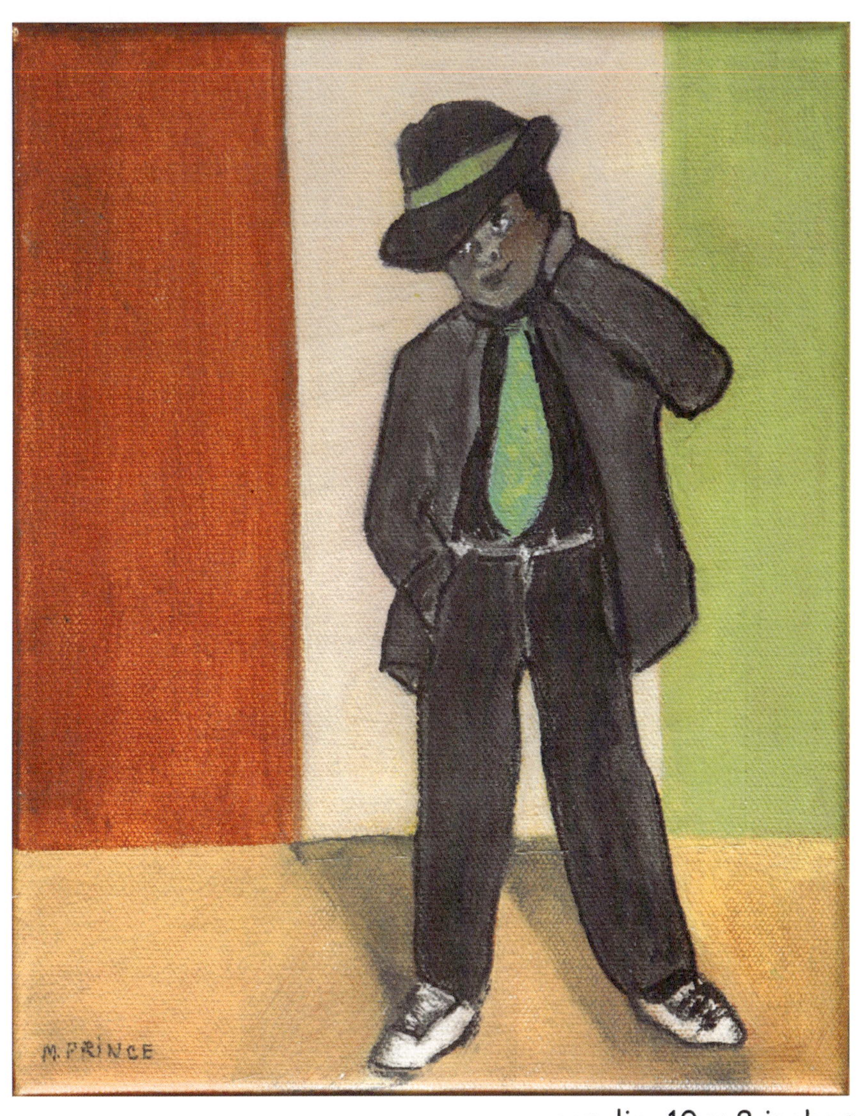

acrylic, 10 x 8 inches

Duo

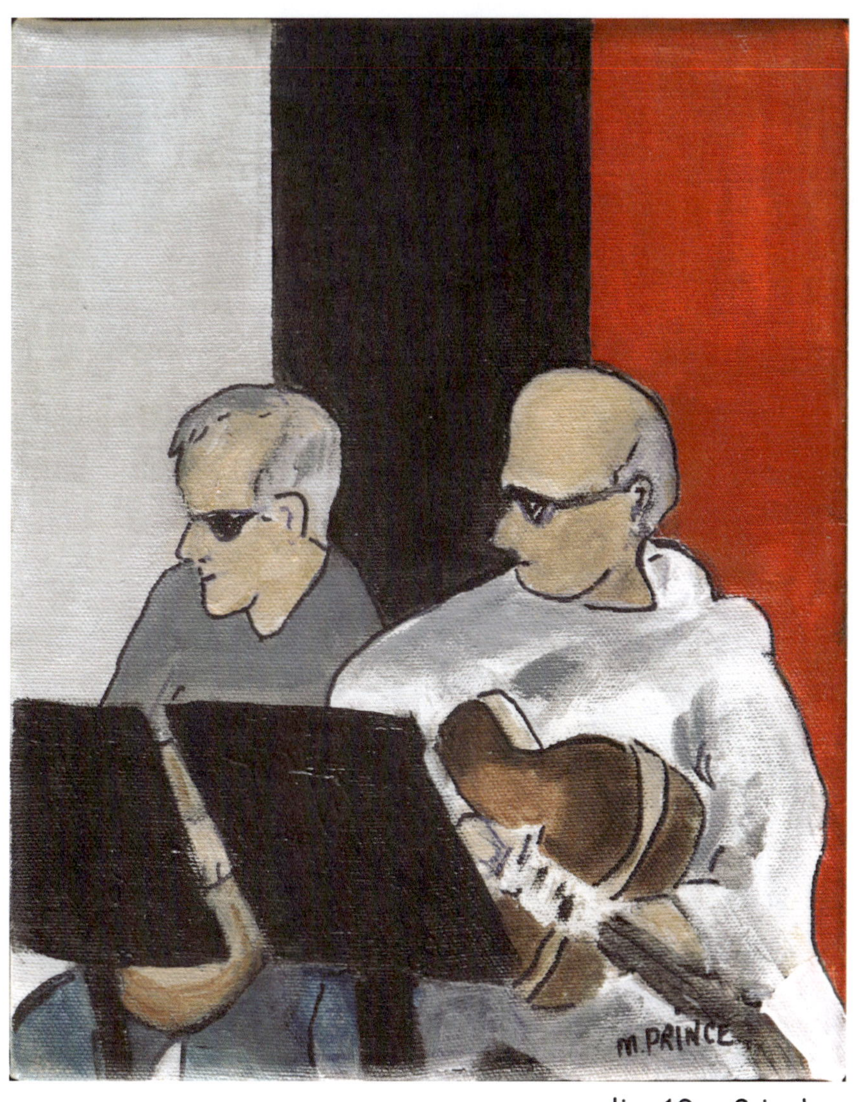

acrylic, 10 x 8 inches

Balance

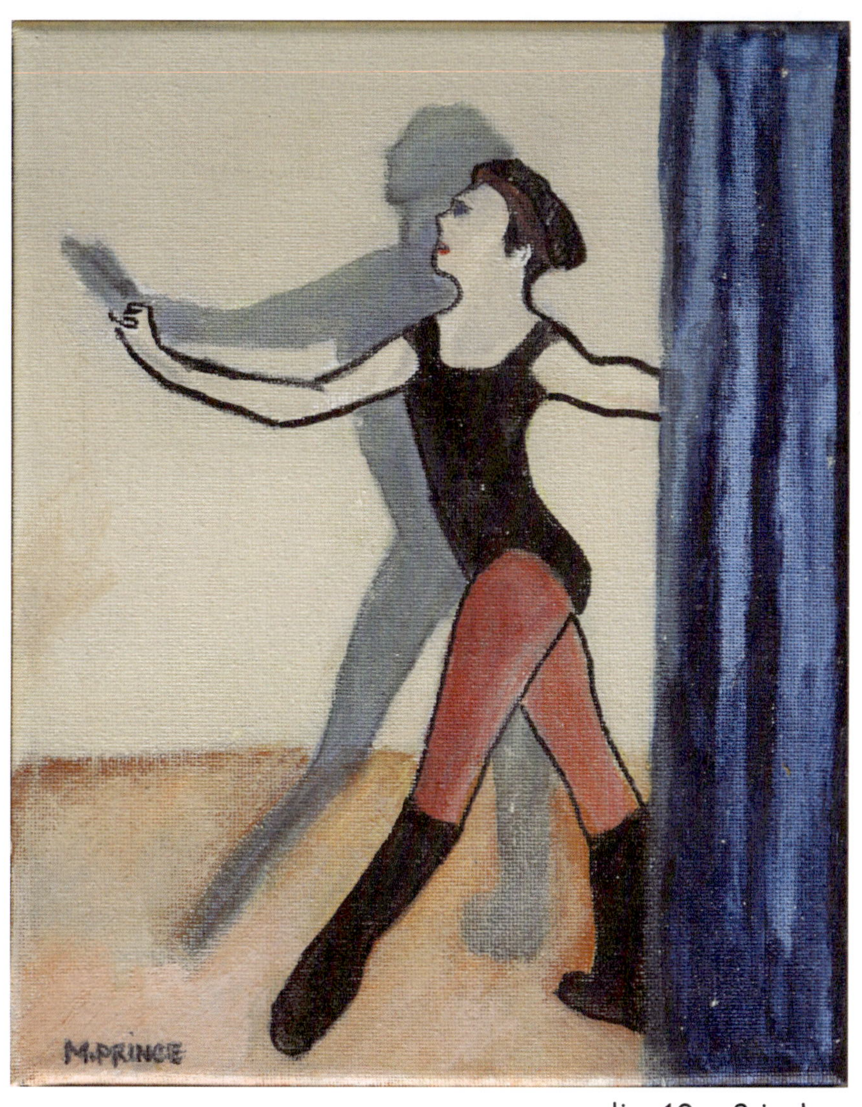

acrylic, 10 x 8 inches

Sax

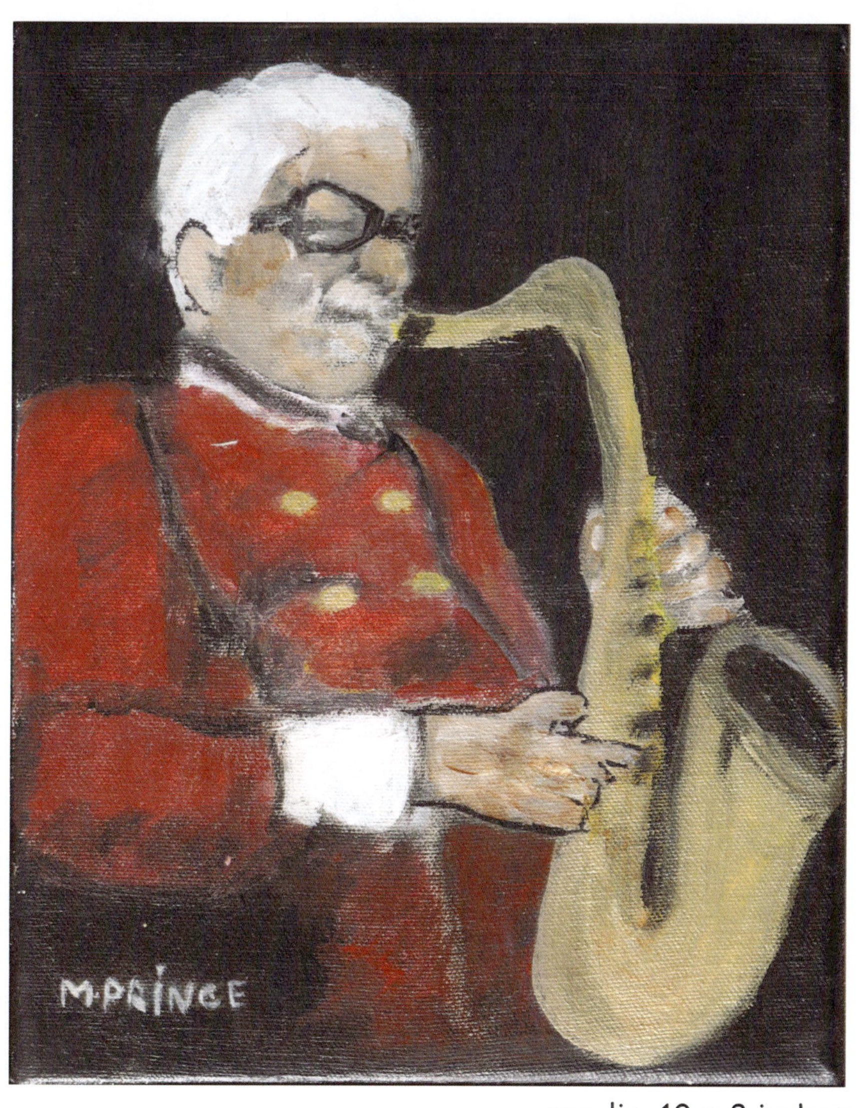

acrylic, 10 x 8 inches

Marionettes

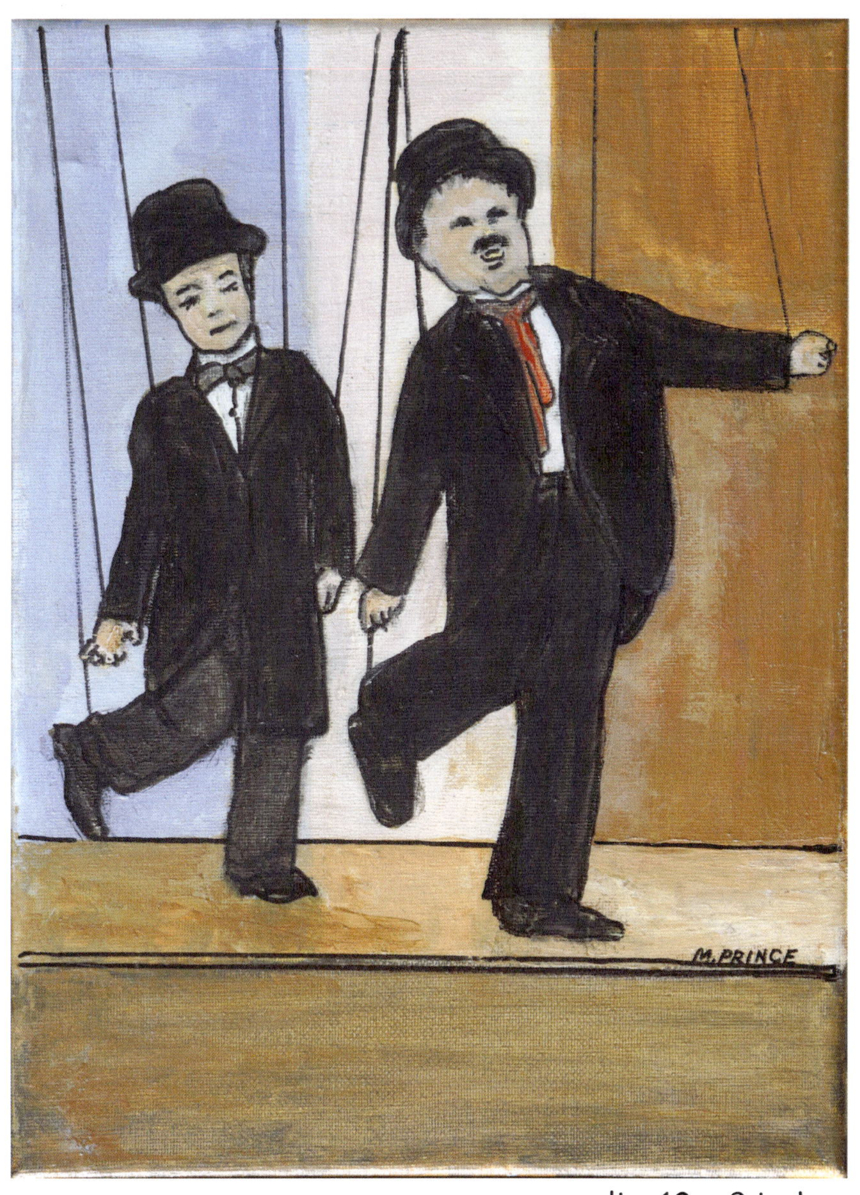

acrylic, 12 x 9 inches

"Taps" on Strings

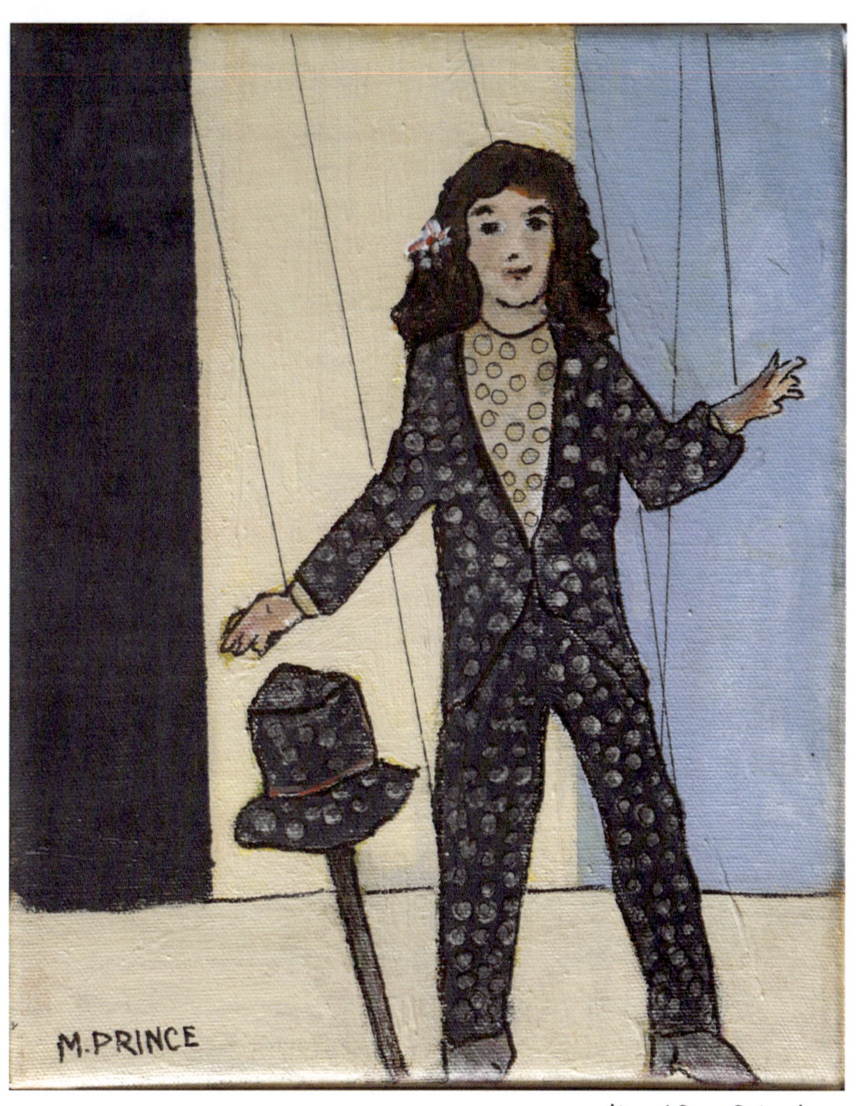

acrylic, 10 x 8 inches

Ringmaster

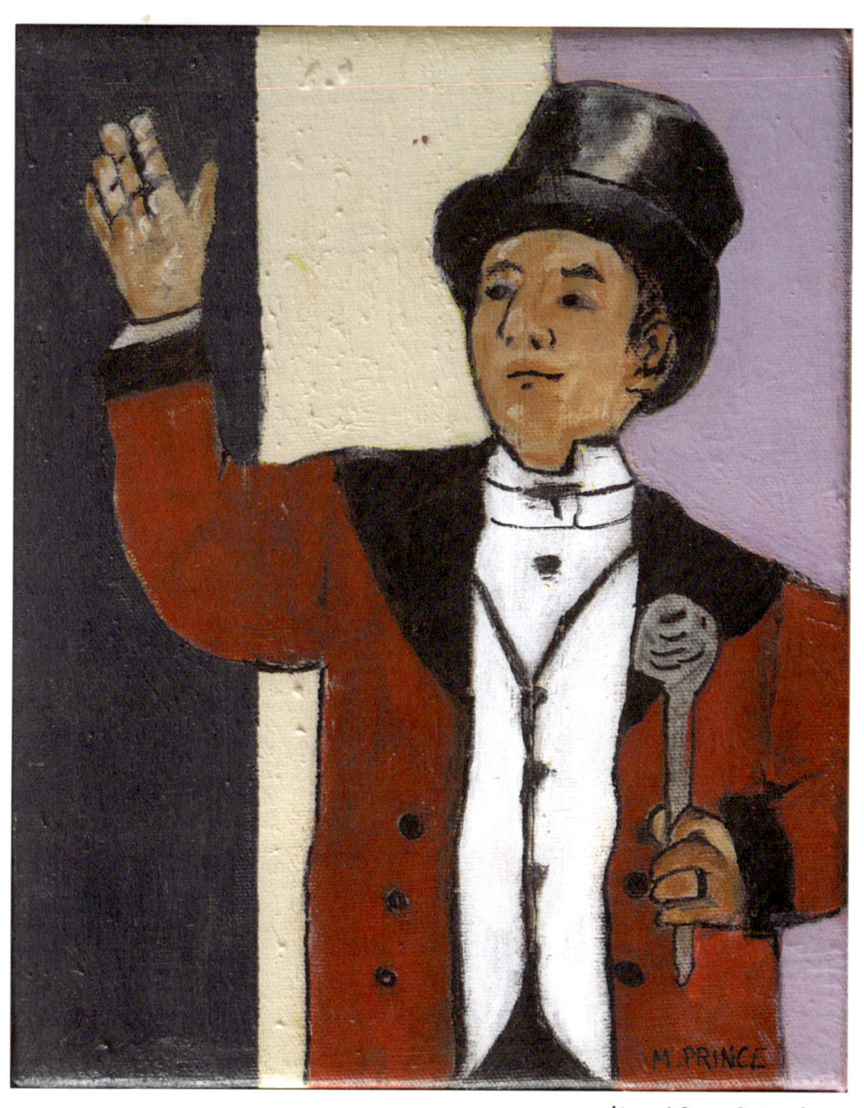

acrylic, 10 x 8 inches

Trapeze Artist

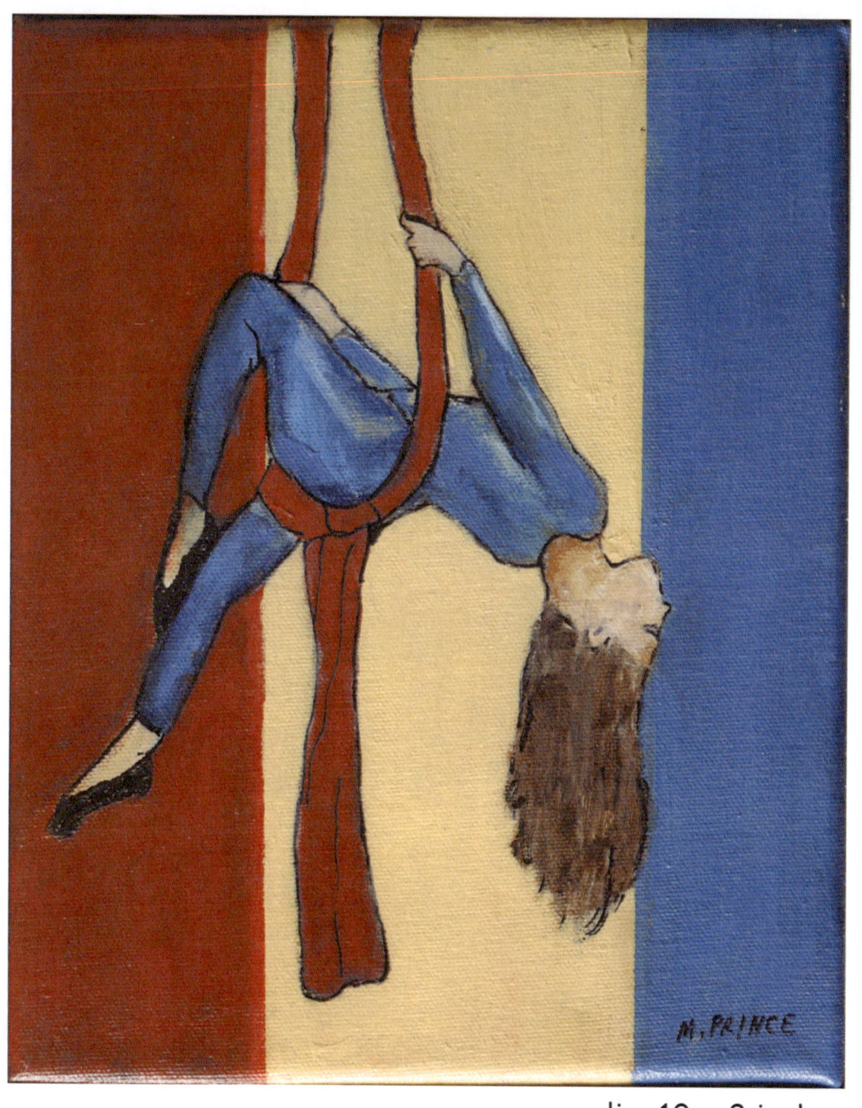

acrylic, 10 x 8 inches

Let's Try

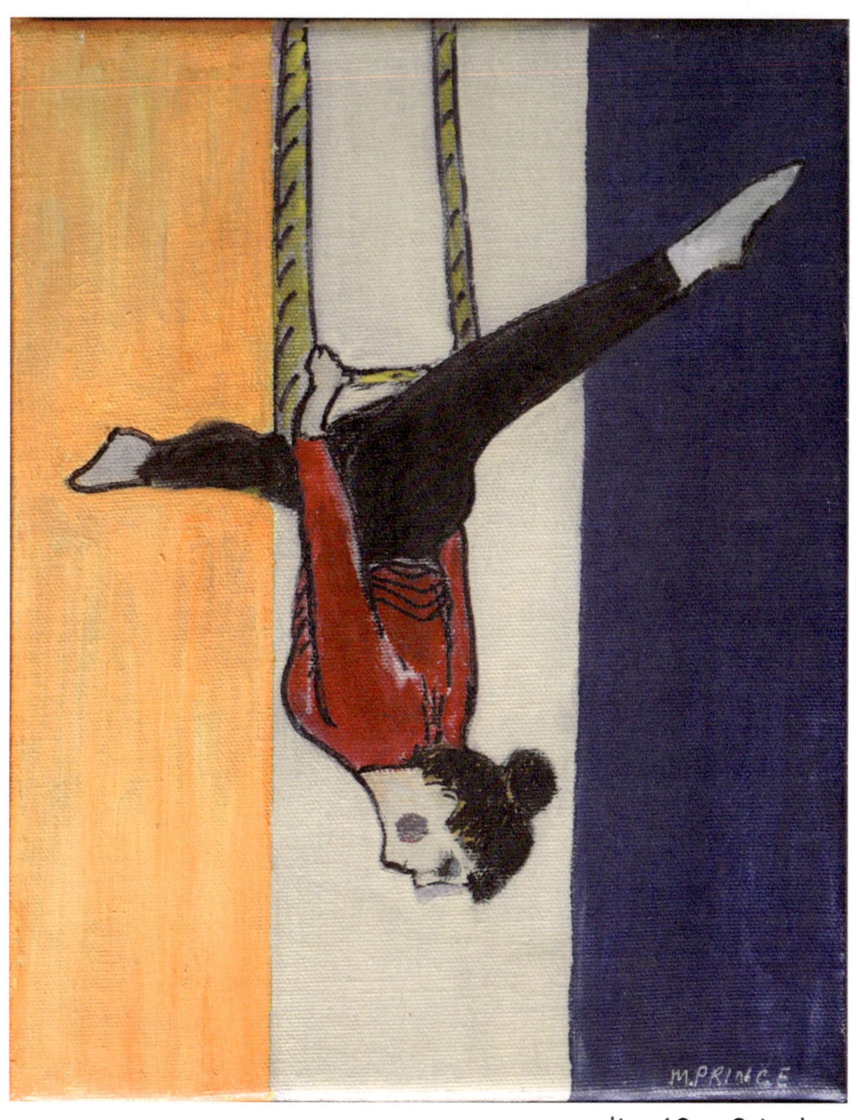

acrylic, 10 x 8 inches

Ship Ahoy!

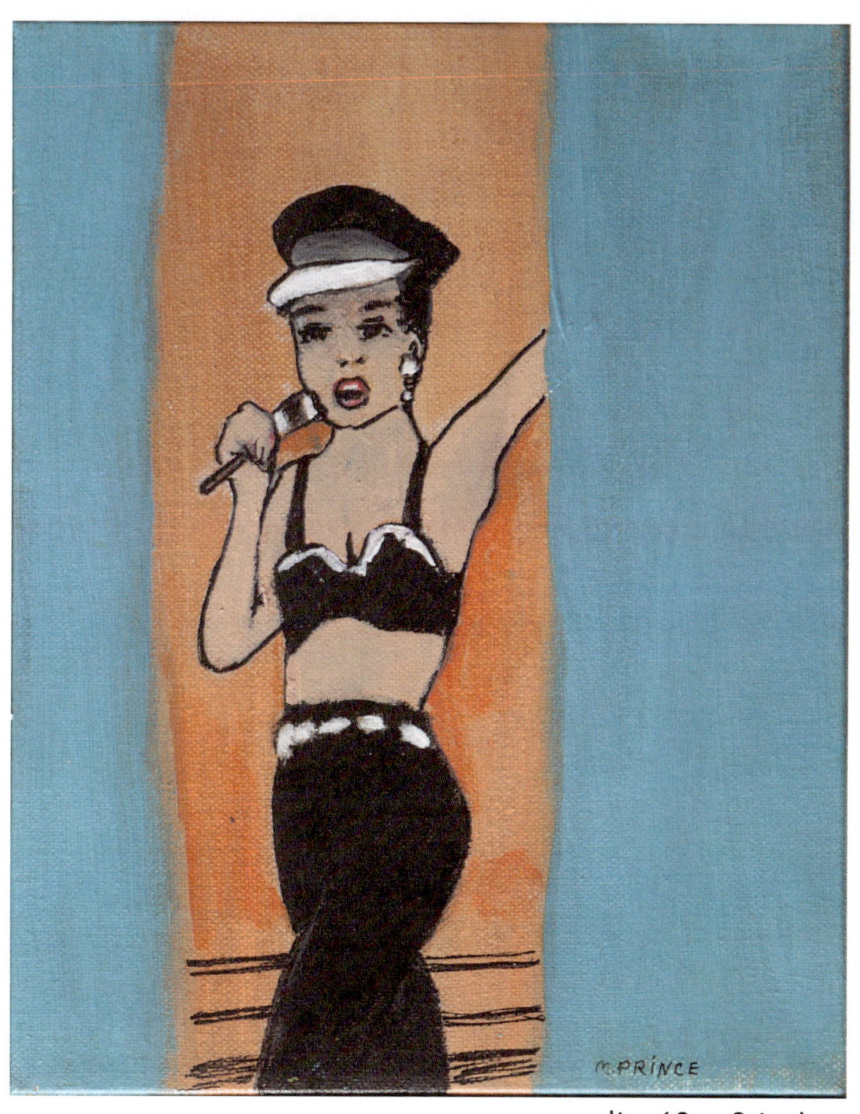

acrylic, 10 x 8 inches

First Performance

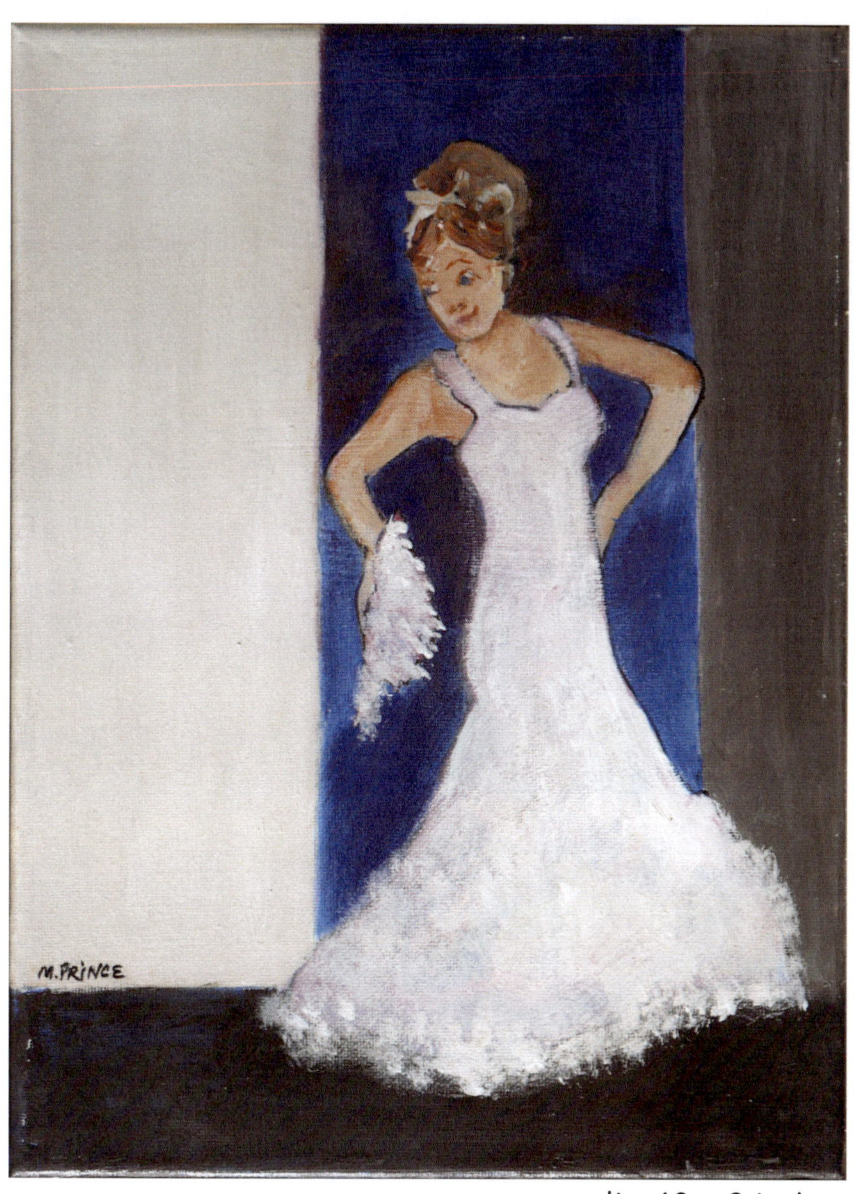

acrylic, 12 x 9 inches

The Actress

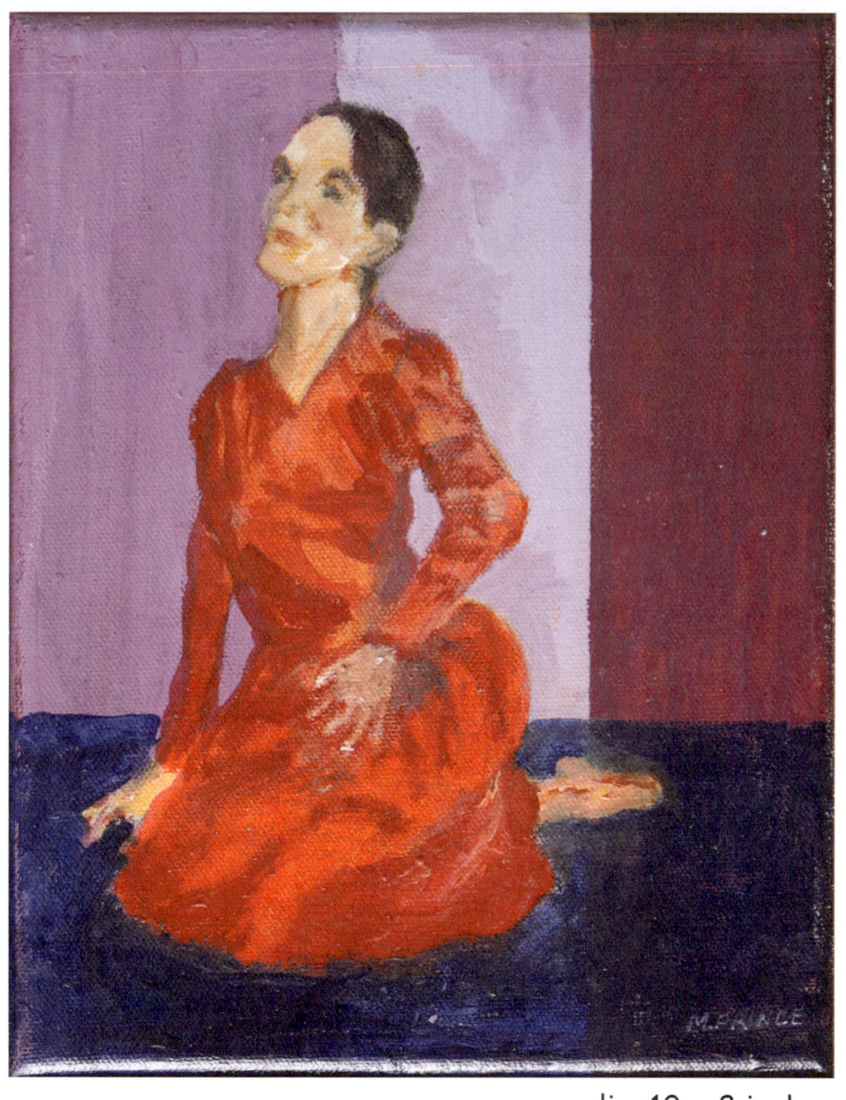

acrylic, 10 x 8 inches

The Way You Make Me Feel

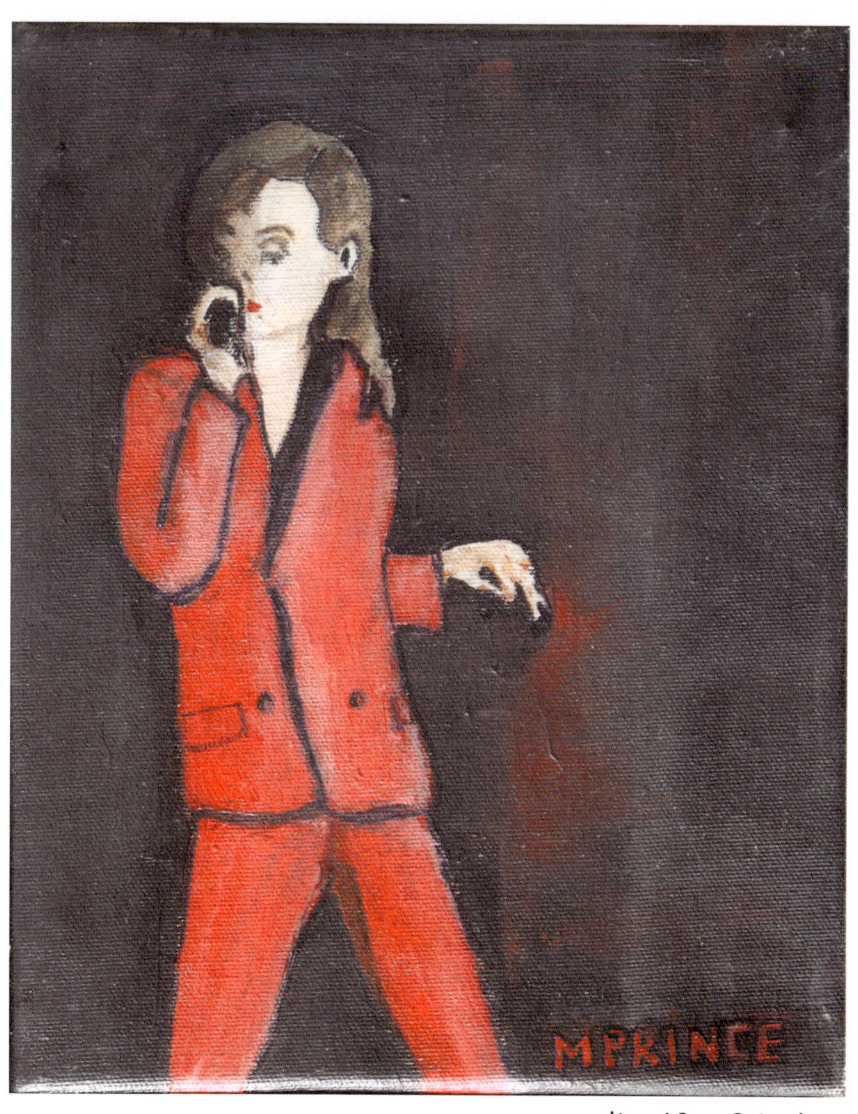

acrylic, 10 x 8 inches

Starlet

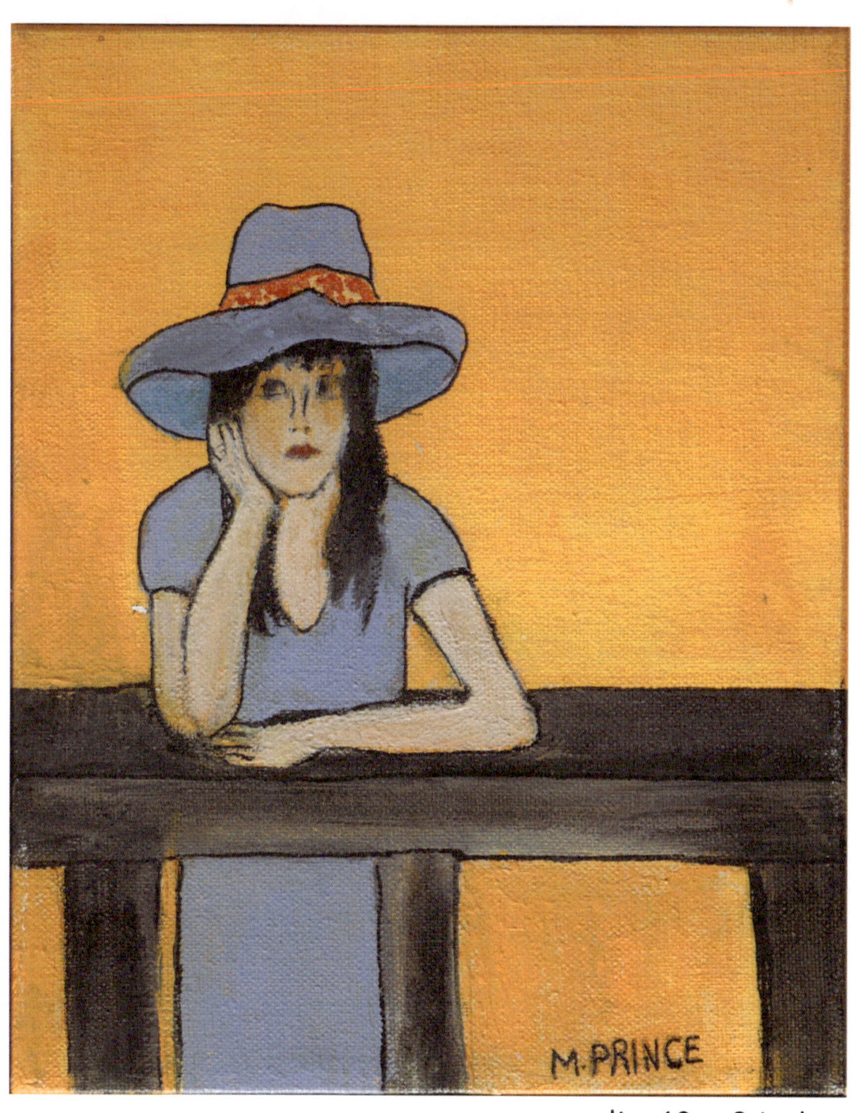

acrylic, 10 x 8 inches

Stage Fright

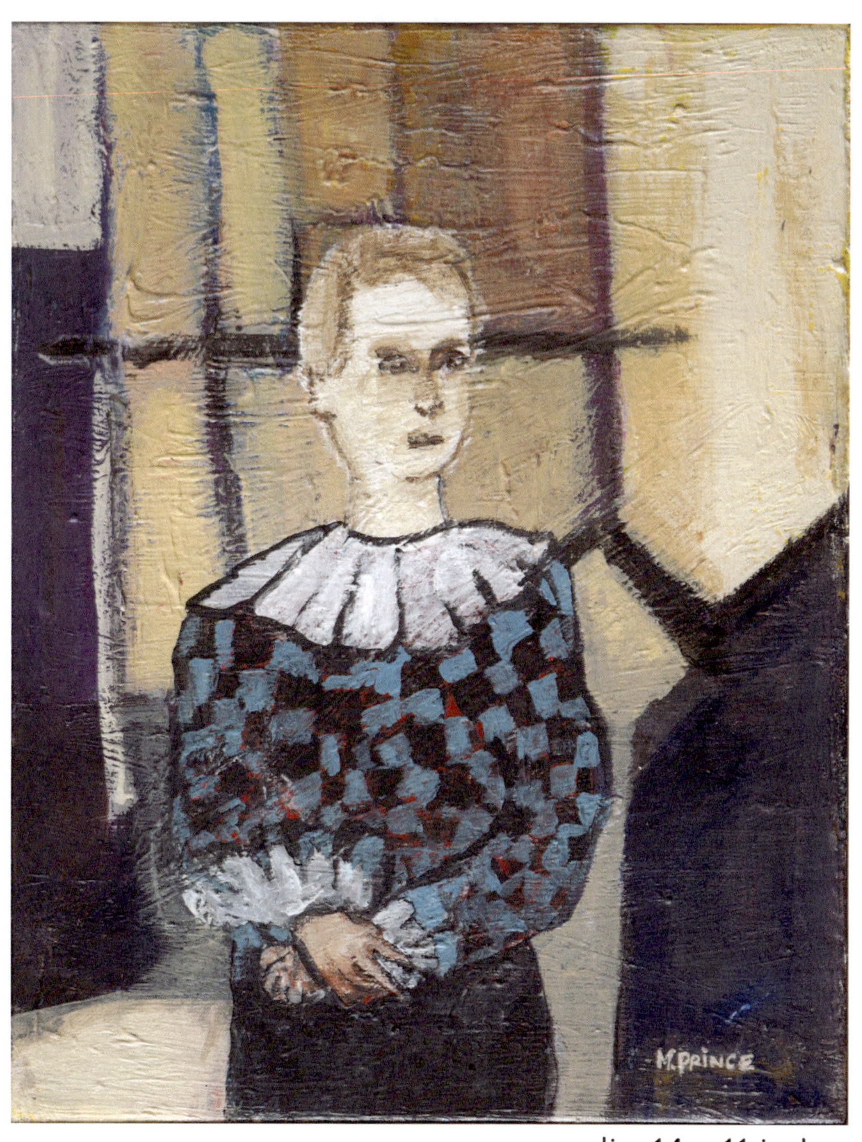

acrylic, 14 x 11 inches

Limbering Up

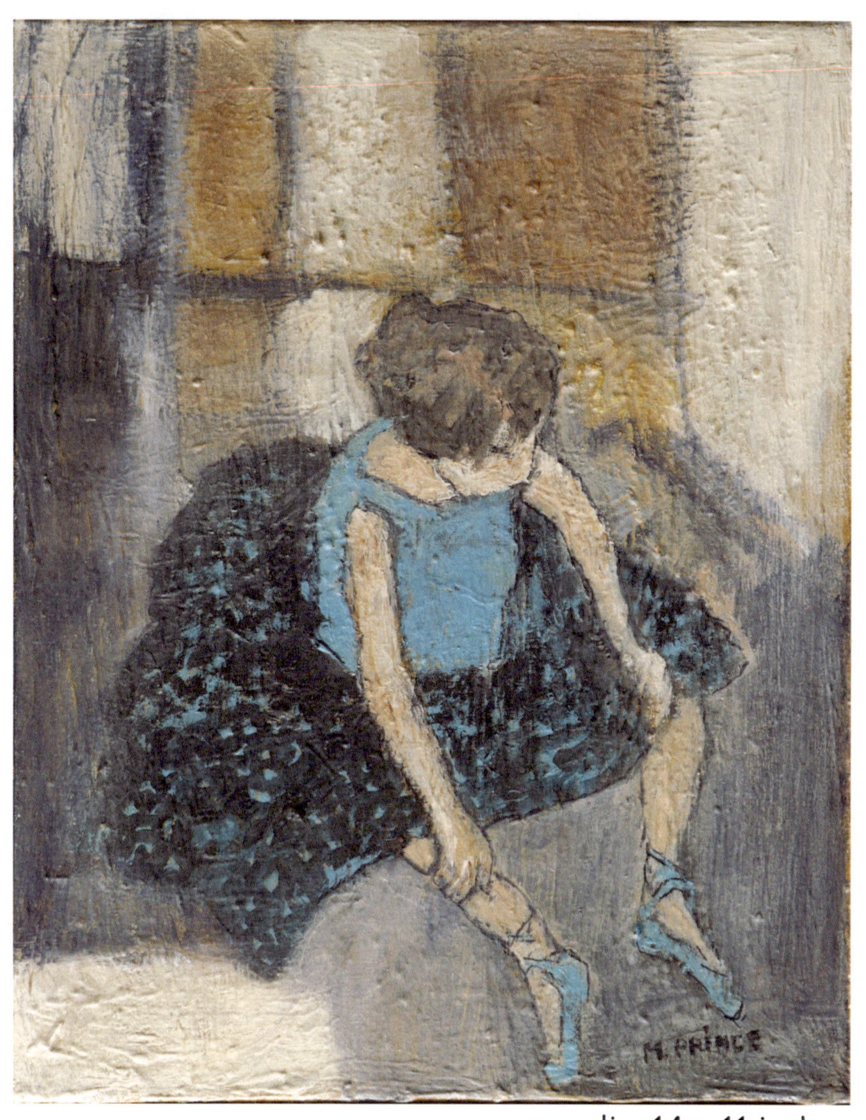

acrylic, 14 x 11 inches

Guitar II

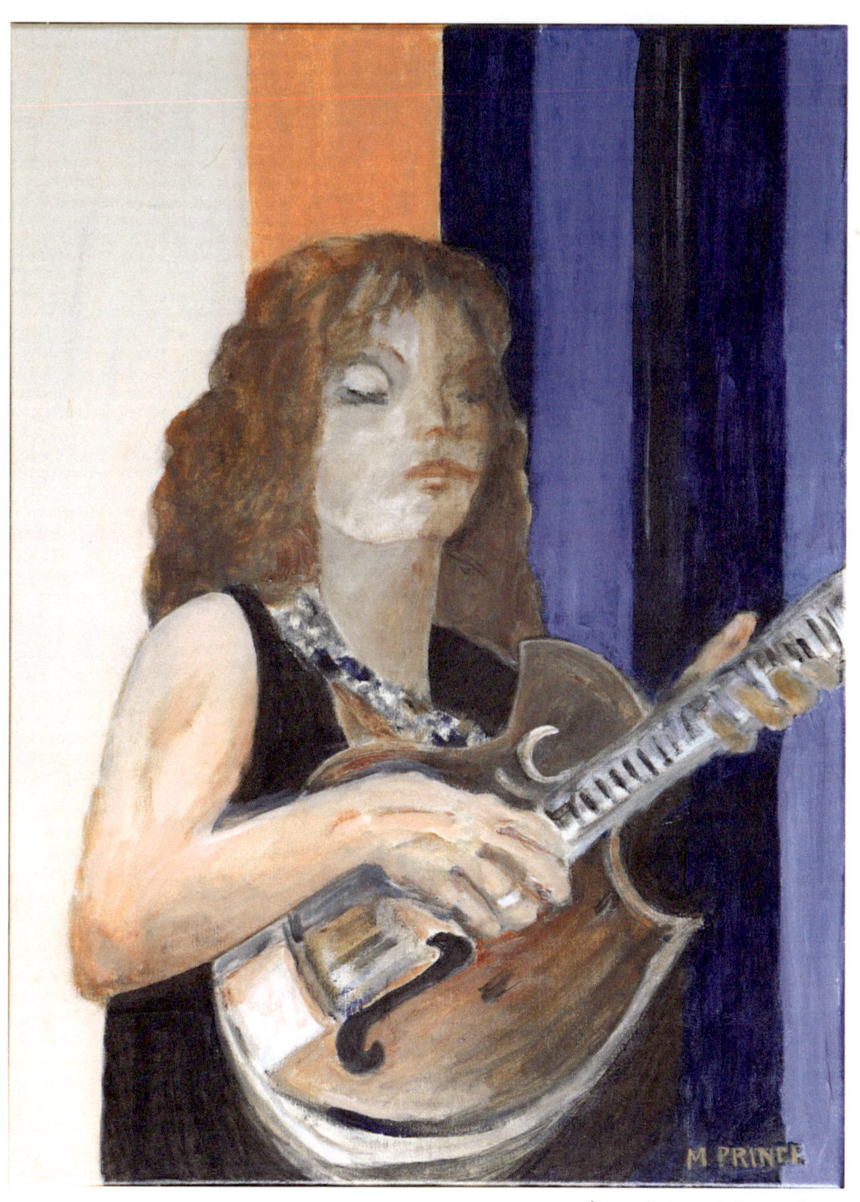

acrylic, 24 x 18 inches

Flute

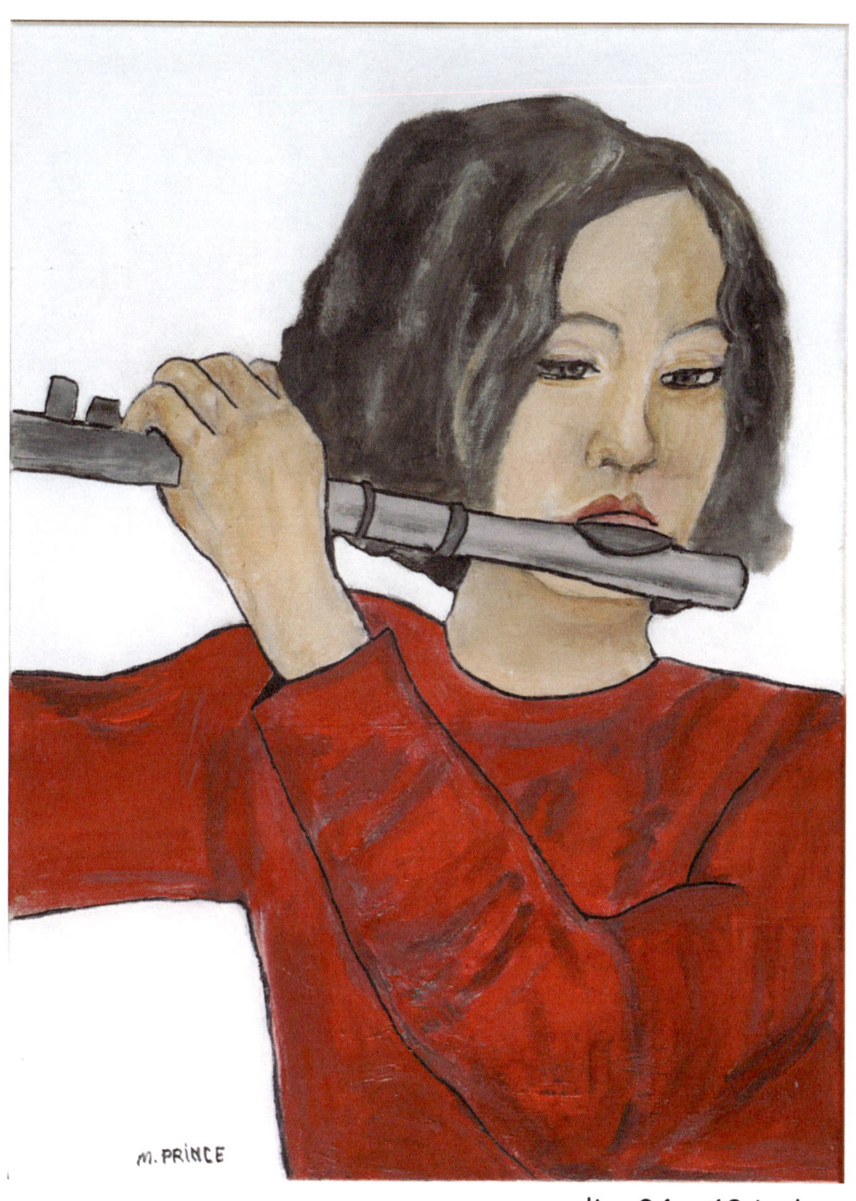

acrylic, 24 x 18 inches

Drums

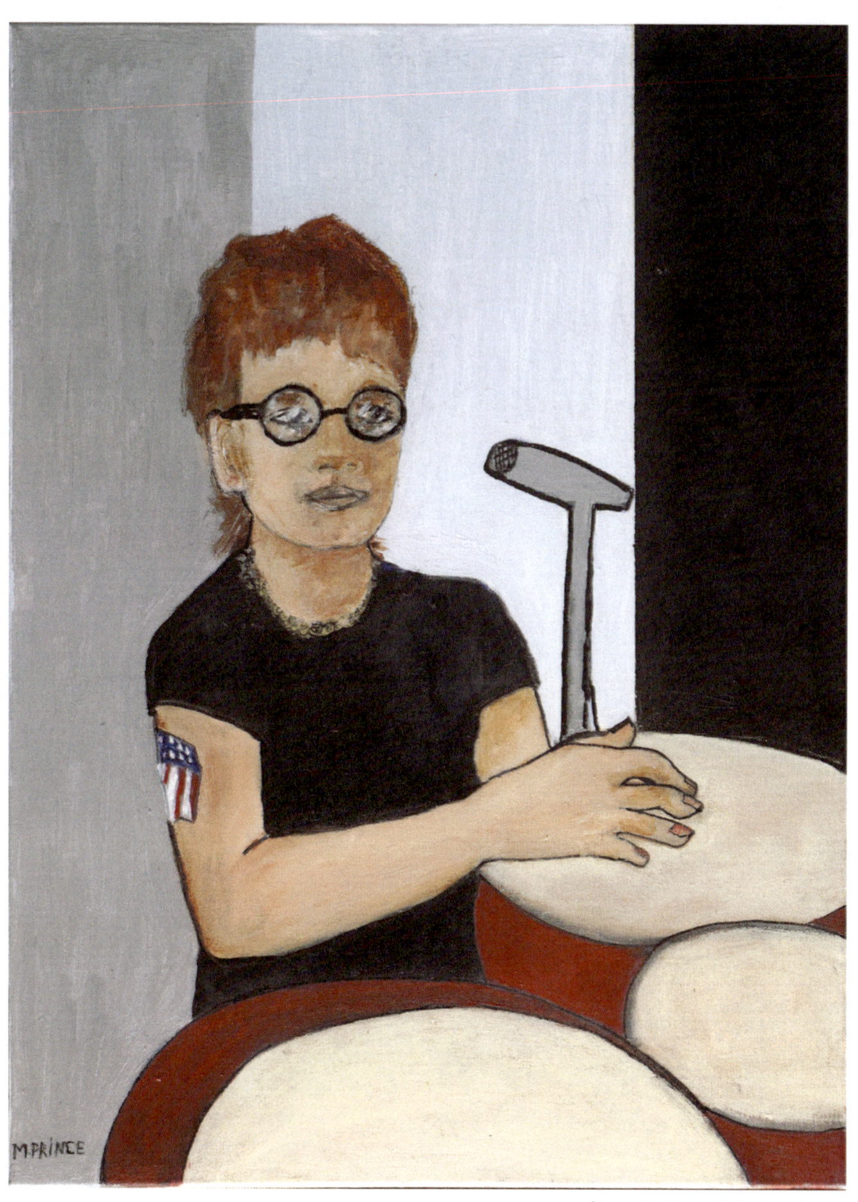

acrylic, 24 x 18 inches

Ballerina

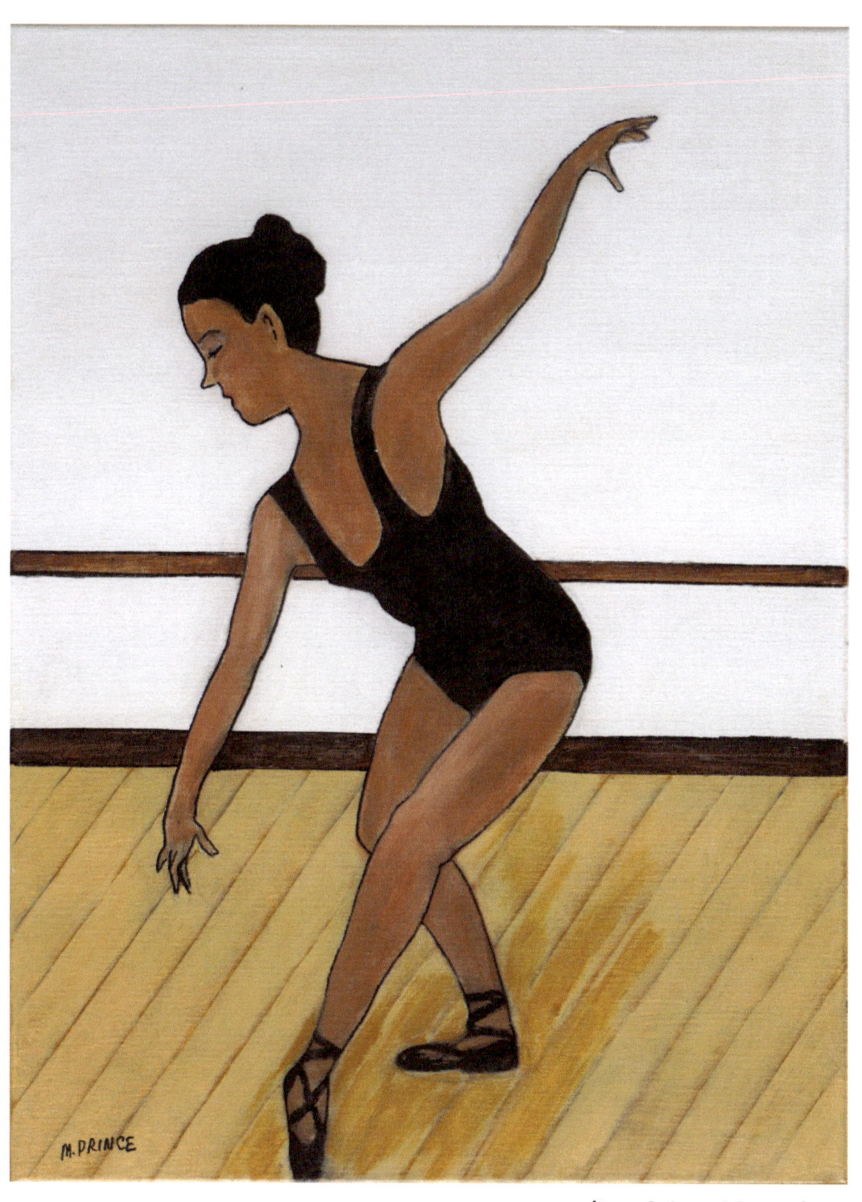

acrylic, 24 x 18 inches

Trumpet

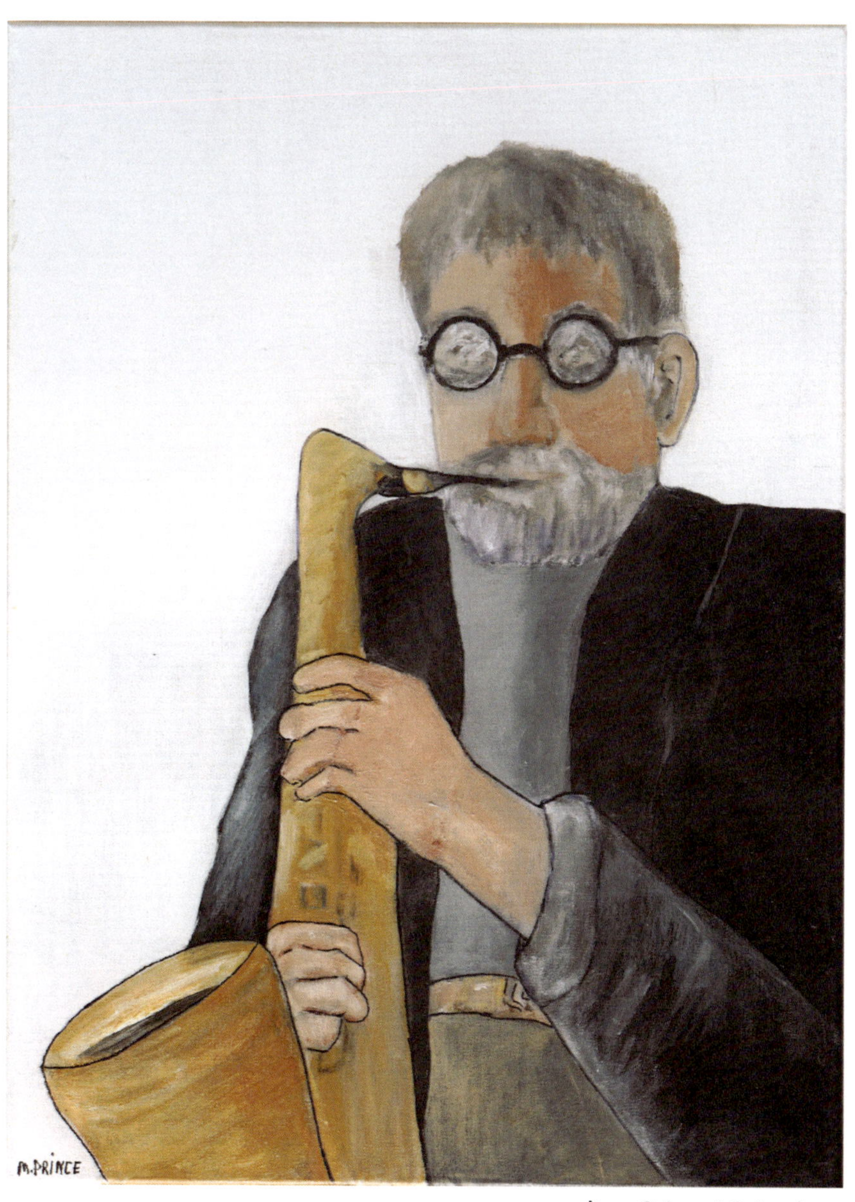

acrylic, 24 x 18 inches

Singer

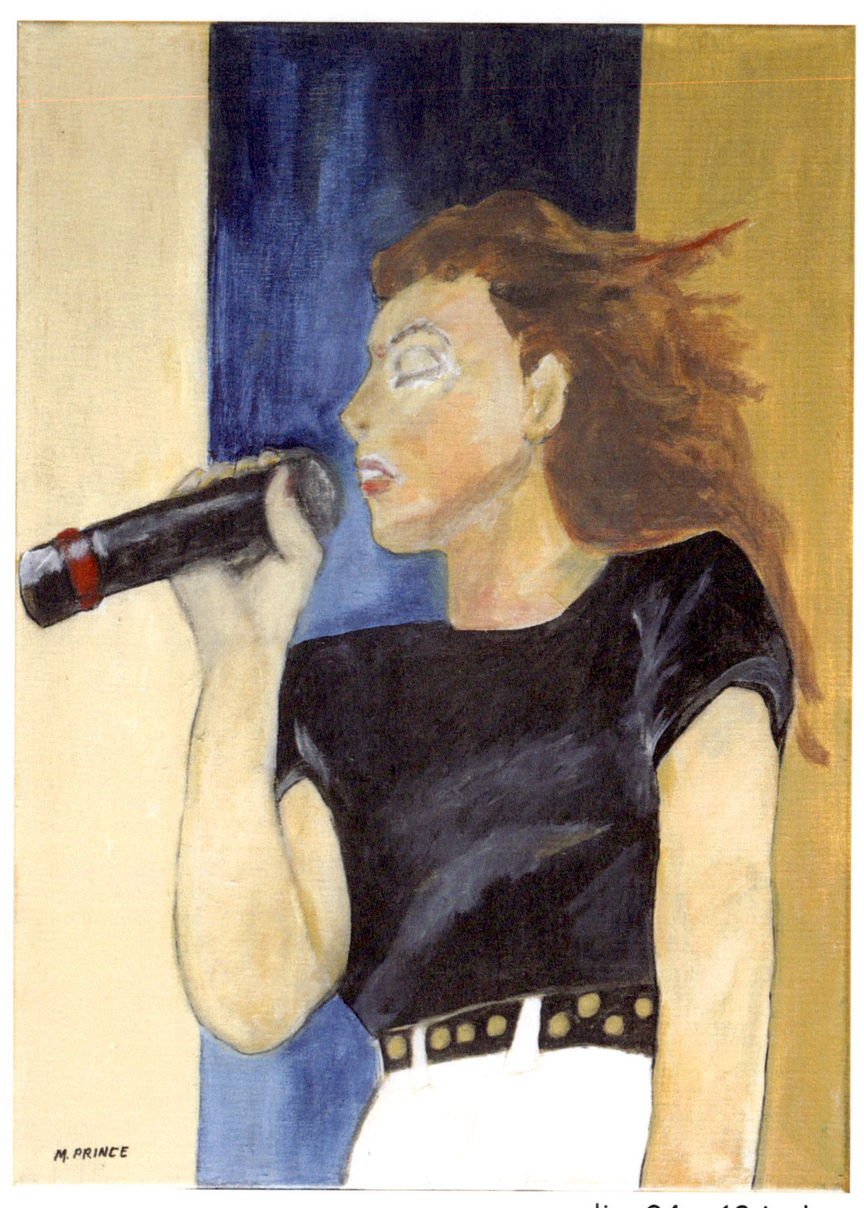

acrylic, 24 x 18 inches

Soloist

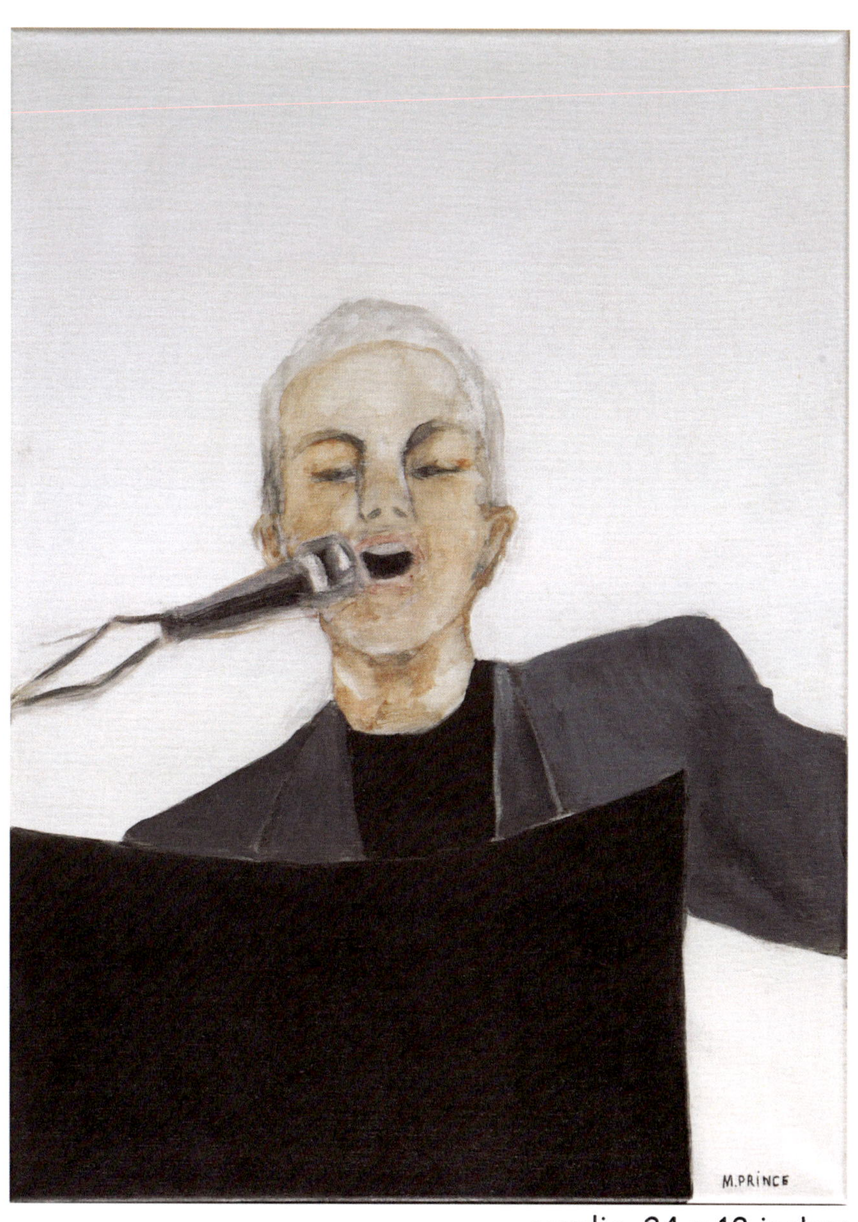

acrylic, 24 x 18 inches

First Night

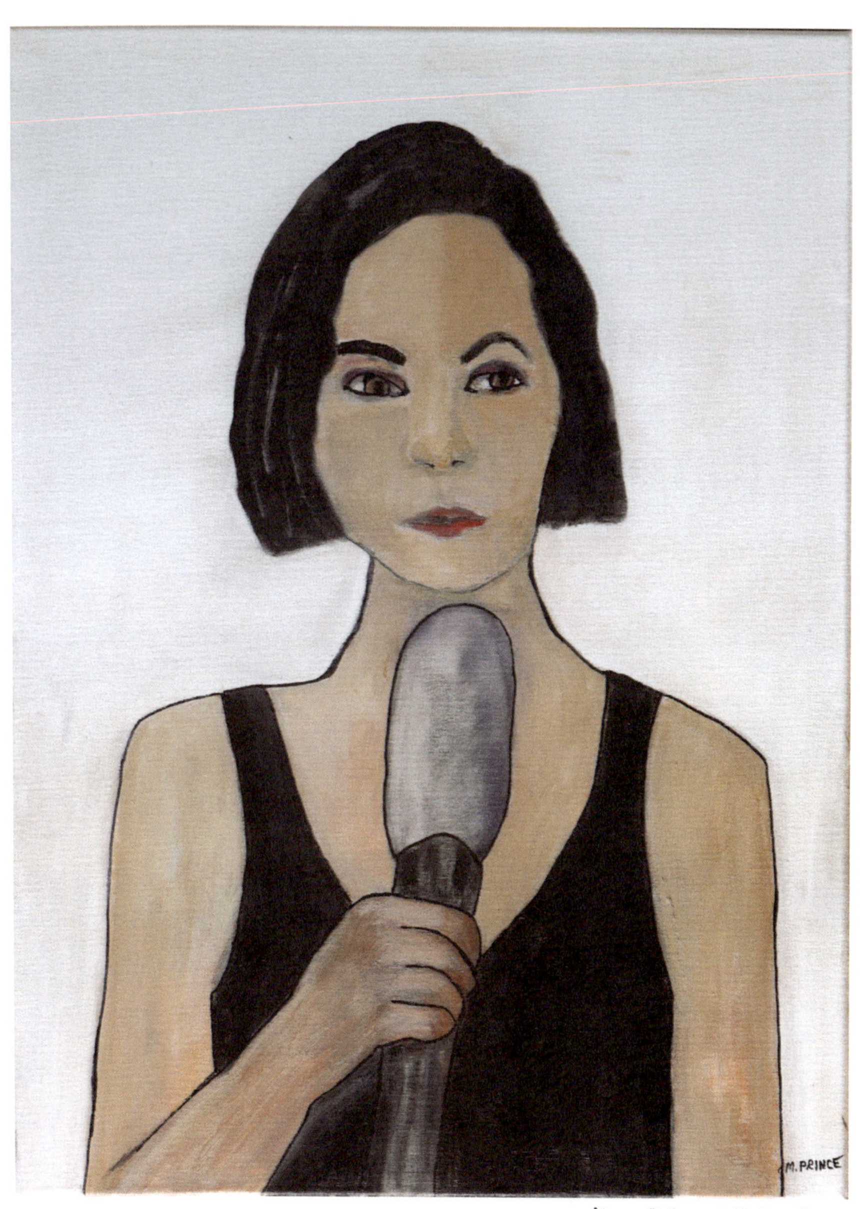

acrylic, 24 x 18 inches